ONE-WAY TICKET TO L.A.

How a Nurse From Ohio Found Love in Hollywood

Barbara Marshall

with Lori Marshall

WAY TICKET TO L.A.
. Nurse From Ohio Found Love in Hollywood

For information, contact Barbara Marshall
onewaytickettola@gmail.com

The views expressed in this book are solely those of the author.

ISBN: 978-1-7354995-0-5 U.S.A.

Published by Sarah Street Press, Los Angeles, Calif.
sarahstreetpress.com

Cover design by Todd Gallopo of Meat and Potatoes, Inc.
Interior design by Jacqueline Gilman, Gilman Design, Larkspur, Calif.

Photo credits:

Cover: Mike Eliason @eliasonphotos

Inside flap: courtesy of the Marshall Family Collection

Back cover: Ron Batzdorff, courtesy of ronbatzdorff.com

Page 197: Michaela Lincoln

Page 206: Dave Allocca/Starpix/REX/Shutterstock (9778066f)
Barbara Marshall and Julia Roberts, Garry Marshall Tribute performance of *Pretty Woman: The Musical*, New York, USA – 02 Aug 2018

All other photos courtesy of the Marshall Family Collection

In loving memory of my husband, Garry,

and the family we created together:

Lori, Kathleen, Scott, Lily, Charlotte, Sam,

Ethan, Emma, and Siena

CONTENTS

AUTHOR'S NOTE: I have tried to recreate events, settings, and conversations to the best of my ability from my memories of them. In a few instances, I have changed the names of individuals to maintain their anonymity—this is only to protect their privacy, not to alter the intent of my story. Not everyone wants to be in the limelight. Welcome to Hollywood.

PROLOGUE

THE FIRST PERSON TO call me the morning we announced that my husband, director Garry Marshall, had died, on July 19, 2016, at the age of 81, was Bette Midler. The phone rang, I picked it up, and I recognized her voice immediately. I said, "Hello, Bette," and then we both started crying.

Garry had directed Bette in his movie *Beaches* almost 30 years earlier, but they had remained friends. More recently, he had directed her daughter, Sophie, in an off-Broadway play called *Billy & Ray* at the Vineyard Theatre in New York. Garry was, quite simply, a wonderful man, and I knew it. Many other people were fortunate enough to have known it, too. Finally, I stopped crying long enough to talk to Bette.

"Will you do something for me?" I asked.

"Whatever you need," she said.

"We are planning a celebration of Garry's life on November 13, which would have been his 82nd birthday. Will you come?" I asked.

"I'll be there," she said.

"Will you sing a song?" I asked.

"Yes," Bette said.

Just a few months later, she stood before more than 2,000 people at the Valley Performing Arts Center, at Cal State University Northridge, and sang "Wind Beneath My Wings" for my husband, Garry. There was not, as they say, a dry eye in the house. It was the perfect song for a man who had brought love, laughter, and joy to so many people.

The fact that Garry was a public figure was sometimes stressful for our children. They had to share him with so many others, people we often called "FOGS," for Friends Of Garry. Some were talented up-and-coming actors, and others were, honestly, just related to his dentist and wanted a cameo in a movie. When it came time to plan his funeral, just days after his death, my children asked that we keep it small, with only immediate family. I felt the same way. Our whole lives we'd had to live with their dad surrounded by actors, actresses, writers, and producers who wanted Garry to give them a job. When it came time to bury him, we wanted it to be just us, his family. We were the people who loved and supported him most, and we had to take our time and say goodbye in our own way.

It is not a mystery how Garry died. He had a stroke on June 27, in the week after a near-perfect Father's Day weekend. The stroke was complicated by pneumonia and possibly a second stroke. He survived in Providence Saint Joseph Medical Center in Burbank for three weeks. The doctors and nurses there were nothing short of outstanding. Garry was alert and responsive, and we were all able to tell him that we loved him, that he would be safe, and that he would be okay. We even showed him old episodes of his TV shows *Happy Days* and *The Odd Couple*, and he laughed. When we showed him a snippet from *Laverne & Shirley*, he made a grouchy face, because that had been a stressful show for him. Typical Garry Marshall—making jokes with his eyes just days before he died. He was always an excellent patient. We were making plans to bring him home. And then, on that final day, July 19, he simply closed his eyes and died, holding my hand and the hands of our three children, Lori, Kathleen, and Scott.

The minute after he died, I picked up his shoes and dirty clothing and said, "Let's go, kids." I grew up the oldest of five children in a Cincinnati family that barely got by, and I'm not one to wallow in tears. I'm a pull-yourself-up-by-your-bootstraps kind of woman, and that is one of the things Garry loved about me. I am a nurse with optimism running through my veins, and he was a hypochondriac who worried all the time about every cough and sneeze. We were the perfect pair, and at that moment I felt so lucky to have been his wife for 53 years. I felt so sad, but I was also so grateful to have been with him for so many wonderful years. We definitely had our difficult times and dark days, as in any good marriage, but in the end, we were still together, laughing and doing the Jumble puzzle in the *Los Angeles Times* together every single morning.

Four days after Garry passed away, we held a small service for him in a chapel at Forest Lawn cemetery. The group included our children and their spouses, our grandchildren, Garry's sisters, Penny and Ronny, and their daughters. The group was so small that only two people signed the guest book, so I threw it away. Garry had wanted to be buried in a coffin, so we chose one with a purple tint, because purple was his favorite color, for his alma mater, Northwestern University. We buried him with some of his favorite things: his St. Christopher's medal, a small red DeWitt Clinton High School duffle bag (which he carried all the time for years!), and his baseball glove. The children wrote notes that they put in the bag. The day he had the stroke, he would not let the emergency room nurse take off his wedding ring. So I let him be buried with it, too.

The children and his best friend, Harvey Keenan, said a few words at the service, and then we followed the coffin to the cemetery plot that Garry had picked out himself several years earlier. There was a fire north of us in Canyon Country that day, and the sky was a brilliant orange as I watched my son, my daughters' husbands, my two grandsons, Penny's grandson, Spencer, and Harvey lower Garry's casket into the earth. The plot he had chosen was under a shady tree, with a bench he had designed and a plaque that read "Sit on it," a phrase from *Happy Days*.

As we stood at attention at the gravesite, ash from the fire flew in the air like confetti as a New Orleans jazz trio played "When the Saints Go Marching In," and, later, Scott led us in singing "Take Me Out to the Ballgame." By the time we had concluded the ceremony, the sun was going down, but the ash was still in the air, and the sky had turned a deep shade of purple. Scott took a picture, because we could not believe the sky was really, truly purple, but it was. Garry was gone from this earth, but he would always be with us in spirit and in our hearts.

With the private, family funeral over, we were faced with the daunting task of planning the larger celebration of his life. Garry worked in Hollywood as a writer, producer, actor, and director for more than 50 years, and to say he had a lot of friends is an understatement. He had thousands of friends. He was a man who felt it was nice to be important but more important to be nice. He made friends with everyone, and they all wanted to come celebrate his life. In the days after his death, men and women would come up to me at events, and even in delis and restaurants, and say to me, "I knew Garry, and I want to come to his celebration." I began to feel uneasy about planning it, thinking it would be in a giant hall filled with strangers I had never met. Yet I felt a sense of obligation and duty to give Garry a big party, because that is what he would have wanted, not excluding anyone.

Finding a location that could hold 2,000 people and was not too expensive was challenging. The producer Bob Boyett, a close friend of Garry's from his television days, said he could arrange for us to have the Ahmanson Theatre, downtown at the Los Angeles Music Center. Unfortunately, the Ahmanson was not available on November 13. We had to stick with Garry's birthday, because he was very superstitious. Traditions, numbers, and signs were very important to him. So we needed to keep searching for a venue.

The Directors Guild, on whose board Garry had sat, offered its facility, but it held only 600 people. Garry loved being a movie director, and he loved being associated with the Directors Guild, because he found the meetings so inspiring. But a venue that small would no doubt leave some people with hurt feelings that they had not been included, so we had to keep looking. Then we found the Valley Performing Arts Center. Coincidentally, Garry had helped break ground for it. I took my children out to see the site, and we thought it was perfect. It was large enough, centrally located, and it meant something to us that Garry had been associated with it.

Once we decided on that, we spent the next few months working diligently to plan the event, with Garry's staff at Henderson Productions (where he worked) and at the Falcon Theatre (a performing arts space in Burbank that he built and ran). It felt worrisome to be doing something so public and big without Garry there to guide us, but we pulled ourselves together to create a beautiful event to celebrate his memory. Scott, who would be the master of ceremonies, dedicated long days and nights to writing his own material, editing film clips, and asking people to speak. Garry hosted events all the time and had grown so comfortable being onstage with a microphone in his hand. Scott did not have easy shoes to fill.

I wore my purple suit, which is really one of the only things I have that is purple, and a pair of black Ferragamo low-heeled flats. Around my neck was the diamond heart necklace from Tiffany that Garry gave me on our 20th wedding anniversary. I used to put it on and take it off, but now it remained around my neck for good luck—Garry had taught me to be superstitious, too. Lori gave me a photo of Garry and me in 1964, sitting on a chaise lounge in Palm Springs, to remind me of happier times. I put the picture in my clutch purse, along with some Kleenex. It was going to be a long day.

We arrived at the theater about 90 minutes before the event was supposed to begin. The children and grandchildren and I snuck in early and saw Bette Midler doing her sound check. This was probably a mistake, because we all started crying. Then I went backstage to the green room to meet some of our speakers. Only in Hollywood would you have a green room at a memorial service. But celebrities always like to have a little drink and snack before a big event. This was a celebration-of-life ceremony, but this was also Hollywood, where things are done differently than in the rest of the world.

I was met with warm, friendly faces and many hugs. I was grateful that the celebration was four months after Garry's death, because it gave me some distance from the shock of losing him. I was able to talk to people openly about him now. The pain was still so fresh, but it was beginning to feel more familiar and safe. Gathered in the small green room were Julia Roberts, Tom Hanks, Rita Wilson, Jeffrey Katzenberg, Marilyn Katzenberg, Michael Eisner, Jane Eisner, Bob Boyett, Henry Winkler, and Hector Elizondo. My children came in, and Kathleen gathered us in a baseball-style huddle. We said, "One, two, three, break," and then we all went into the theater.

Julia Roberts wanted to sit next to me, because she had come alone. She took my hand and led me to our seats. I had known her since she was 21 years old, when Garry directed her in *Pretty Woman*, in 1989. She was now 48 years old, the married mother of three young children. After *Pretty Woman*, she and Garry worked together three more times, on *Runaway Bride*, *Valentine's Day*, and his final film, *Mother's Day*. Julia is a true friend, and nobody was prouder of her success than Garry. For a movie star, she is about as real and genuine as it gets in Hollywood.

When the celebration began, it was as if my son, Scott, was channeling Garry, and we were all thrilled to see him onstage. His comedy timing and material was pure Garry Marshall. There was a giant hole in our lives now that Garry was gone, and though nobody could fill it, Scott made us laugh in the same way Garry could make an audience roar. As I sat in my seat, I kept thinking of what Garry would have thought of this event. He would have said, "Make sure there is good parking, don't feed people but give them a snack, and don't make it too long." Garry's worst fear in life was to bore people. The celebration of his life was anything but boring.

Tom Hanks, Julia Roberts, Jeffrey Katzenberg, and Michael Eisner each took the stage. Scott had been worried about Katzenberg and Eisner appearing together, because they had had a falling out years earlier, when Katzenberg had resigned from the Walt Disney Studios and cofounded DreamWorks Animation. But when Scott called to ask about the situation, Jeffrey said, "It's fine. This is about your dad, not us." Paris Barclay, president of the Directors Guild, also spoke beautifully about Garry's contributions to film. Scott had made sure that wonderful home movies and video clips were woven through the program. In the audience were Billy Crystal, Richard Gere, Julie Andrews, Dick Van Dyke, Helen Mirren, John Stamos, Jennifer Garner, and more. It almost felt like the Oscars, but nobody won or lost.

At the time of his death, Garry had been working on a musical version of *Pretty Woman*. He and its screenwriter, J.F. Lawton, had written the book, producer Paula Wagner and director Jerry Mitchell had signed on, and singer-songwriter Bryan Adams had composed the score. Now Bryan sang the love song for us. It was a wonderful way to announce that the production was moving forward and honor Garry's memory at the same time.

In the final half hour, Bette Midler made everyone cry with the song I had asked her to sing, "Wind Beneath My Wings." Garry used to say that no one should cry in a movie or play unless it was important to his character. I think in this case, all the tears in the theater were legitimate and heartfelt. Lori and Kathleen spoke about the loss of their dad, who loved long walks, frozen yogurt, naps, softball, ketchup, and writing nice letters on his personalized stationery. Kathleen announced that Garry's Falcon Theatre would now be the Garry Marshall Theatre. In his will, he had asked that it be renamed, and we were honoring that wish.

I joined my children onstage and we brought up Heather Hall, Garry's beloved assistant for more than 20 years. Together, we thanked everyone for coming. Then we had a surprise: The Northwestern marching band appeared from backstage, thanks to two more of Garry's friends, Morty and Mimi Shapiro, the president of Northwestern and his wife. Since graduating in 1956, Garry had been a big supporter of the school. All three of our children graduated from Northwestern, as well as our granddaughter Charlotte. Garry had sat on the board of directors, and together we had donated money to dedicate buildings in our name for television and film studies and a dance center in the name of Marjorie Ward Marshall, Garry's mother, who taught tap dancing in the Bronx throughout Garry's childhood.

The NU marching band was the perfect way to wrap up the wonderful celebration of Garry's life. For the next several hours, the children and I hugged and kissed all our friends and thanked them for coming. The next day, both Billy Crystal and Richard Gere called

Scott and told him what a great job he'd done hosting the event, and that meant a lot to us.

And then it was over. Lori flew back to San Francisco with her family. Scott returned to Malibu, where he lives with his family. And Kathleen and her husband and daughter went back to their house, just a few blocks away from my own. I made a cup of tea, exhaled a sigh of relief, and wondered what was next.

When Garry was at St. Joseph, I'd talked to him a lot about what was happening to him. He was only capable of responding with his eyes, but I knew he understood me. I told him that if and when he died, I wanted him to stay in touch and let me know he was still watching over all of us. We always used to talk about the fact that if one of us died before the other, that person should come back and visit the other one. It sounds like a joke, but we really did talk about that kind of thing. One of the last things I said to him was "If you come back, knock something off the wall so I know it's you."

The weeks after the celebration were a blur. Letters and flowers continued to pour into my house as the new normal of my life began. The year ahead would be filled with cleaning out Garry's closets, donating his films to Northwestern, and organizing not only his production company but also the new theater. I tried to keep up with some of my normal routine. I got my hair and nails done once a week. I went to yoga classes in the lobby of his theater once a week. And each morning, I got the newspaper and did the Jumble, just as Garry and I had for so many years.

Then, the week before my 78th birthday (March 9, which also would have been our 54th wedding anniversary), a little miracle happened. I woke up and walked down to breakfast. When I was about to pass through our dining room, I noticed shattered glass, a lot of it. I have a lot of plates hung above the fireplace in our dining room, and the plates hang over a shelf of teacups and saucers. One of the plates had fallen. It was a souvenir from the Empress Hotel in Victoria, British Columbia, where Garry and I had taken the children in the 1970s. I knew immediately that Garry's spirit had knocked the plate off the wall. He was sending me a clear message that he was still with me. I picked up the fragments and smiled.

Garry had written two books with our daughter Lori about his career. He knew I was writing this book, and he was very supportive. We talked about it and what it might look like; I read him drafts of some of the chapters during the last years of his life. Lori and I had started and stopped working on it many times, because life just got busy. And after Garry died, I just felt too sad to jump back into it again. But six months went by, and suddenly I found myself ready to tell my story.

Garry was a master storyteller, and over the years he stole a lot of material from my life to use in his television shows and movies. Now it is my turn—to convey my story not through the eyes of my husband but through my own eyes. The journey from the backwoods of Cincinnati to the red carpets of Hollywood was not an easy ride, but I wouldn't trade a moment of it.

CHAPTER ONE

MY LIFE BEGAN IN quite an ordinary way and somehow became quite extraordinary. I have always been an extremely positive person, but there are plenty of positive people who don't have dreams that come true. If you look back over the narrative of my life, you would not believe that I would one day meet not only Julia Roberts and Julie Andrews, but also Bill and Hillary Clinton and Barack and Michelle Obama. My childhood was about as far from show business as a person's could get.

I was born about seven in the morning on March 9, 1939, at Mercy Hospital in Hamilton, Ohio, to Vivian Lorraine Billington and James Edward Wells. It was my dad's 26th birthday. My mom was not yet 20 years old. It was not a poor beginning or a lavish beginning. It was simply the day I was brought into the world and named Barbara Sue Wells. My parents said it was just a name they liked, and there had never been a girl named Barbara in either of their families. So it was a name all my own.

My parents had been living in Hamilton for about a year. My dad worked at a bakery called Kirk's, making $14.85 a week. He took out $5 each week to pay for a furnished apartment. When my mother went to the grocery store, she would spend about $4 and fill so many bags that she couldn't carry them home. For an extra dime, a grocery clerk would deliver the bags for her. It was the end of the Depression and near the beginning of World War II, and a lot of things were different then.

When I was born, my mom was in a six-bed ward and stayed in the hospital for nine days, even though there were no complications, which was usual in those days. She got to take me home on March 17, St. Patrick's Day. On her morning breakfast tray was a green shamrock napkin, which she took home as a keepsake. One of the things my mother preferred to forget about that day is that when my dad arrived to pick us up, he was drunk. He said he felt celebrating the birth of his first child was a reason for drinking. Unfortunately, my mother didn't agree. He stopped drinking that day and didn't start drinking again until he retired.

Both my parents came from large families, which was pretty common in the rural Midwest during the 1920s and 1930s. My mom, Vivian, was born on June 29, 1920, in Chickasha, Oklahoma, to Clara May Underwood and John Pettis Billington. She had five sisters, and the birth order was Pauline, Louise, Marie, Helen, Vivian, and Johnny Lee, who was given a boy's name to continue the family tradition of naming a child *John* in every generation. My grandpa Billington was a bootlegger, and my grandma Billington made extra money taking in other people's laundry and ironing. She once ran an ad in the newspaper that read "Ten pounds fully starched and dried for 59 cents."

My dad, Jim, was born March 9, 1913, in Irvine, Kentucky. He grew up one of 11 brothers and sisters. There would have been 13, but two of his siblings died young, which wasn't infrequent in large families back then, due to inadequate medical care. My dad was the third youngest, and the birth order was Merdy, Ben, Noe, Hilliard, Maud, Ella, Ruth, Sue, Jim, Avery, and Lucille. Their father was a Baptist preacher who also ran the general store.

My parents met under the most unromantic of circumstances—in the mouth of a dead whale. It was part of a big sideshow, and everyone in Chickasha wanted to see it. The whale had washed up onshore somewhere and it weighed 48 tons. It was traveling around the Midwest in a boxcar to towns along the railroad. Locals found the whale so fascinating that some couples opted to get married in front of its mouth, thinking it would bring them good luck.

My mother went to see the sideshow with her sister Louise, and a guy named Pickles let them in for free, because they didn't have enough money for two tickets. While the centerpiece of the show was the whale, there were other attractions as well. One boxcar contained an octopus; another, a girl dressed as a mermaid; and another, a variety of dead fish considered exotic to the Midwest.

My father was one of the men traveling with the sideshow. He took one look at my mom and was fascinated by her bright red hair and freckled peaches-and-cream skin. He asked one of his coworkers to see if she would go on a date with him. The coworker told my dad to speak up for himself.

She was standing beside the whale looking into its mouth when he asked her out on a date. She was only 17 years old, while he was 24, and she was immediately attracted to his fancy navy suit and the big roll of money that he carried. She quickly agreed. He told her to come back when he got off work at 10 p.m., and he would take her out. Later that night, he took her to a hamburger place. Not long after that, he left the circus and returned to Ohio. Vivian joined him in Hamilton, and they got married. They were together for the next 70 years.

She got pregnant with me right away. Being pregnant at 17 might seem young by modern standards, but in the late 1930s it was not uncommon for someone with Vivian's background to get married and pregnant so early. None of her sisters graduated from high school or even thought about going to college. Their parents divorced when Vivian was eight years old, and the family dispersed, living with friends and relatives around the Midwest. She was a roamer. Whenever someone got mad at Vivian, she would leave and find a new place to live. Being married to Jim and pregnant with her first child at 17 looked like the promise of a stable future.

We lived in Hamilton, Ohio, until I was two years old. Shortly after my second birthday, however, Kirk's bakery was forced to close, because the owner wasn't paying his taxes. My dad found a job at Cincinnati Valley High Bakery. We quickly moved to Cincinnati to be closer to his work.

At the new bakery, Dad was paid $25 a week. That was more than he had ever been paid, and my parents felt like they were suddenly rich. They rented an apartment on Maple Avenue and even had enough money to buy furniture. They bought a used bedroom suite, a table and chairs, and a stove and set up their first real home.

A year or so later, they moved to another apartment, on Elm Street near a music hall. By now, World War II was in full swing, and men like my dad, who were married with small children, were not the first to be drafted. That's the first home I remember. My best friend was a boy named Dexter, who lived with his parents, Bea and George, across the street from us. Dexter was 13 years old. I had just turned three, but I liked to hang out with him because I had no brothers or sisters. His grandmother lived with them, and she would sit in their front window every day reading the Bible. She once told me the longest word in the Bible was *Nebuchadnezzar*, who was the king of Babylonia and conqueror of Jerusalem. She used to try to teach me to spell the word, but I never could get it right.

I liked being an only child. I had a little table and chairs where I would have tea parties with my dolls. There was a big park across the street where I often played. We lived on the first floor, and I was free to walk through the neighborhood alone during the day, even though I was only three years old. Other kids also wandered around the neighborhood without their parents, because it was considered safe. On the corner was an Italian restaurant. Sometimes I would go to the restaurant and sit in a booth with the owner and watch him make meatballs. Today I can make excellent meatballs, and this is perhaps why.

When I turned five, we moved again. This time it was to a better neighborhood, on Delhi Road off River Road, so that I could be in the district to go to Harrison Elementary School for kindergarten. I walked to school by myself, because by this time both my parents had jobs. Dad continued at the bakery, and my mom had gotten a job at a company called Aluminum Industries, which made pistons and other supplies for the war. For extra cash, my dad took on a job at a trucking company. He worked at the bakery in the morning and helped load supplies onto trucks late at night.

My parents were often so tired when they came home from work, they would simply eat and go to sleep. Before I went to bed, if she was not too tired, my mom would roll up my curly hair and pin it with bobby pins to keep it from getting frizzy while I slept. Then, in the morning, my mom would brush my hair out. One morning, however, my mother was too tired to brush out my hair. When I gave her the brush, she kept falling asleep with it in her hand.

I ended up having to go to school with my hair a complete mess. I didn't know until I got there that it was picture day for the kindergarten class. I looked so shaggy and was so embarrassed that my hair was not straight and perfect, like all the other girls in the class. Half the time I felt like I was raising myself and, for the most part, not doing a very good job of it.

Despite our hectic home life, we did manage to have fun together. My parents used to take me to the Rialto movie theater on Friday nights, when they had an amateur hour before the movie. A neighbor made me fancy formal dresses, and on some nights, I came out onstage with a microphone and sang. Much to my surprise, I would win every time we went to the Rialto.

My parents, Vivian and Jim, in Hamilton, Ohio, in 1938, shortly after getting married.

First prize was $3, which was considered quite a nice prize for a little girl in kindergarten. I beat out acrobats, ballet dancers, and tap dancers by singing songs like "You Are My Sunshine" and "Sentimental Journey."

After my wins at the Rialto, my mother thought I had a future as a performer, so she hired a manager for me. He put together a troupe of four little girls, and we would perform on radio shows and at different restaurants around town. I remember singing atop a table at one restaurant and thinking it was nothing but fun. My mother called a friend who was a newspaper reporter and asked her to write an article to help promote my career. The headline billed me as "Cincinnati's Own Shirley Temple." There was only one problem, and it was a big problem: I couldn't dance.

This picture was taken on March 9, 1944 to commemorate my fifth birthday. Some people thought I could become "Cincinnati's Own Shirley Temple." Unfortunately, I could never dance.

My mother tried to sign me up for tap-dancing lessons, but the teacher told her to save her money. It turned out I simply had no rhythm, and because of that had a limited future as a dancer. As luck would have it, my performing career was put on permanent hold when I was eight years old and my mother decided to have another child.

The day the baby came home from the hospital marked the one and only time I ever missed school. I had a perfect attendance record and was proud of it. But when my parents brought home my new baby brother, Jimmy Dale Wells, I left school at lunch and didn't go back that day.

With a new baby in the house, my mother had no time to take me to singing auditions. Time got tighter when she started having more babies. When Jimmy Dale was a little over two, my sister Gloria was born, and when Gloria was 19 months old, Stephen was born. When Stephan turned six and I was a senior in high school, Brenda arrived and completed our family. My mother was pregnant in my graduation photos, which seemed to overshadow the fact that I was the first person in my family to graduate from high school.

Before all the kids were born, Mom and I used to shop regularly for new clothes. But once the four other kids arrived, there would be no new clothes. We would still get dressed up and go downtown shopping, but we could only window shop. We didn't dare go into the stores for fear the clerks would make a mistake and think we wanted to buy something. I would stand outside the stores looking in the windows and daydreaming that someday I might have money to buy new clothes again.

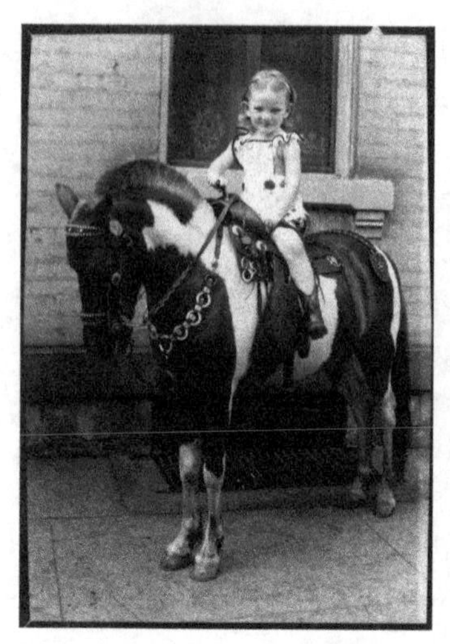

One day a man came along and offered to take pictures of the kids in our neighborhood on a little horse. This was around 1943.

When I was growing up, we never had a car. So whenever we saw a nice car, we would take a picture standing by it, to make the background more interesting. Half the time, we had no idea who the car belonged to. It was not until I moved to Hollywood that my parents finally bought a car.

This 1944 photo is of my first-grade class. I am standing in the front row, four in from the right.

With my parents around 1943, still an only child who wore a lot of bows in her hair.

In 1943, this picture was taken by a professional photographer to celebrate my fourth birthday.

With my dad on Easter Sunday, around 1945.

With my mom at the Cincinnati Zoo, also around 1945.

CHAPTER TWO

I THOUGHT MY TEACHERS were the most wonderful people in the world. They not only unlocked doors to new worlds for me, they seemed to have the kindness and patience I hoped to master when I grew up. My parents and my friends' parents had blue-collar jobs that were long on hours, short on wages, and left them completely exhausted by the end of the day. My teachers had stable jobs with reasonable hours that left them invigorated. I couldn't think of a better job than one where you got to work with children and books.

I went to Harrison from kindergarten through sixth grade. My second-grade teacher was named Miss Brunswick, and she was the most elegant woman I had ever met. Her parents died in an accident shortly after the school year began and left her an inheritance. One day she came to school in a brand-new black Packard. When I saw her driving that car, I thought I'd never seen any woman look as pretty as Miss Brunswick. She wore silk dresses and straight skirts, and every so often she had a new hairstyle. The class thought she looked like someone right out of the movies.

My third-grade teacher was Miss Schneider, who lived with her mother. In her classroom stood a beautiful bookcase containing volumes of leather-bound books. They were collections of poetry. The books were alluring yet forbidden to us. We were only permitted to stare at them, because she never took them out of the case. She said that someday we would be old enough to appreciate poetry, but that third grade was too soon. That made the books all the more appealing to me.

One day I mustered the courage to ask Miss Schneider if I could try to read one of the poetry books. She knew I was a serious student and so, after thinking about it, she said that if I remained in the classroom during lunch hour, she would leave me alone with one of the books. She locked the door so that none of the other students could get in.

Once alone, I read through one of the poetry books. I was in heaven.

She continued to let me stay inside during lunch for the rest of the year. From that day on, I just loved to read books. I not only liked the words, I liked the look of the words on the paper, the binding, and the cover art. I couldn't wait to dive in and let the words take me away on an adventure. Every time I pick up a new book, even today, it seems like the first time I sat alone with a book in Miss Schneider's classroom.

My fourth-grade teacher got sick in the middle of the year, and she never came back. Some students speculated that she might have gotten pregnant, but we never knew for sure. That happened a lot: Teachers would disappear, with no explanation given to the kids. They thought we were too little to understand about such problems, so they just swept them under the carpet. One teacher would leave, and another would arrive, without so much as an assembly, a good-bye party, or even an announcement.

That was the year our class read *The Secret Garden.* I thought it was the best book ever. It was the first one I read cover to cover all by myself. It was exciting and dramatic, the first of many books that showed me how people lived outside Cincinnati. That was also the year we began going to the school library. It was my favorite day of the week. I loved bringing home new library books and diving into them the moment I got there.

Toward the end of fourth grade, my world came tumbling down when I got scarlet fever. In those days, it was thought to be deadly, because it could affect your heart. So immediately after I was diagnosed, officials from the public health department came to my house and put a *Quarantine* sign on the front door. They permitted my dad to go to work, but my mom and I, as well as my little sister and brother, were not allowed to leave the house or accept any visitors. Someone from the public health department came once a week to check on us. I couldn't go back to school until I was well again, so I sat inside with a high fever watching blotches grow on my body. It was such a sad and lonely time.

One of the signs that the disease was over was when the blotches on your hands started to peel. Some parents even used sandpaper to speed up the process, but we did not. My case lasted six long weeks. Finally, the public health department said I could go back to school, under one condition: Some officials followed me into the school and made me clean out my desk and burn all my books. They thought germs might contaminate the other students. I didn't have a lot of books, and the thought of having to set fire to any of them just killed me. I'll never forget the stern look on the faces of the health department officials as they watched me toss my books into the school's incinerator.

Once my problems in fourth grade were over, I cruised into fifth grade. My new teacher, Miss Ruck, wasn't as strict and straitlaced as my previous teachers had been. They were all very particular about how you sat and how you wrote, but Miss Ruck was a new breed of teacher. She also was the mother of a young son. And she talked to us about this new invention called television. Many of the kids had TV sets at home, but we didn't have enough money to buy one yet. When my friends came in talking about *The Howdy Doody Show*, I didn't know what they were talking about. I felt like the odd girl out, but Miss Ruck protected me during those times and was especially nice to me. Eventually, my family got a round 12-inch television set. It sat in the living room, and I was so happy to have Howdy Doody in my house.

Along with our schoolwork, Miss Ruck taught us practical things. She said you should always have a safety pin with you, because you never know when you are going to lose a button or otherwise need one for a quick fix. She kept hers tucked inside the waistband of her skirt, and I started keeping one in my skirt, too. I thought Miss Ruck was just a terrific teacher and a well-put-together person. She was smart, practical, and knew how to handle any situation that came her way.

At Harrison, classes were large, but we knew most of the kids. Nobody came from very far away, and most kids walked to school. The neighborhood was very clean and there was little crime. When we got home from school, we would have a snack and sometimes listen to the radio before going outside to play.

On Sundays, we would all go to church together; sometimes my parents would send me alone, because I enjoyed it so much. The first church I ever went to was a Baptist church with a children's choir. Sometimes the kids would get together and have a garage sale to benefit the church. We didn't have the sale in our neighborhood. We knew nobody would want to buy our old stuff, because they had old stuff just like it in their houses. We would go downtown to a church in a very poor neighborhood and set up our sale there. We also sold greeting cards and hosted potluck dinners to benefit our church.

After graduating from Harrison, I moved on to nearby Oyler Junior High. It was in a primarily black neighborhood, and some of my friends' parents wouldn't let their kids go there, because they were not ready for integration. Some parents found ways to send their kids to other schools in the area. My parents didn't have any money to move to a better neighborhood, so I wound up going to Oyler for three years. From my perspective, we were poor, but the kids at Oyler were even poorer. It didn't matter what color they were.

It was good for me to see a neighborhood other than my own. And it was an important school for me, because at Oyler, teachers started asking me about my dreams beyond high school, which was not something my parents ever talked to me about.

I continued to have wonderful teachers, some bordering on eccentric. For example, in the eighth and ninth grades, my speech teacher: She would be talking about public speaking and look down and lament the fact that her nail polish had chipped. It became routine that I would sit on a stool beside her and paint her fingernails as she taught the class. She later shared some of her beauty tips with me, such as how to apply lipstick to make your lips look fuller. She said that would help me because my lips were so thin. My mother wore a lot of makeup, but she never had time to teach me any beauty tips.

Some of my other teachers were all about academics. If I had to choose one who changed the course of my life, it would have to be Miss Budke, my eighth-grade English teacher. Sometimes I think that if I hadn't gone to Oyler, I might never have met her, and I wonder where I would have ended up.

Most of the students in our class did not like Miss Budke, because she was very strict. I enjoyed learning what her rules were and abiding by them, because they made sense to me. This didn't help the fact that I struggled academically in her class. I tried hard, but I usually got Cs on my tests and papers. On the rare occasion that I got a B, I was thrilled. I couldn't read very fast, and spelling was always hard for me.

That year, the board of education administered a standardized test. A woman stood with a stopwatch at the front of the room, tapping her pencil and giving us words to spell. I remember one of the words was *roof*. For the life of me, I couldn't figure out how to spell it. Then she used it in a sentence. "The *roof* of the house was red." I couldn't picture it or sound it out. My mind just went blank.

Later, we had to write a social studies paper on a famous person. I couldn't come up with anyone interesting. Then my teacher happened to mention that the king of England had just died, and his daughter Elizabeth would now be queen. My teacher was able to get me some newspaper clippings from England about the coronation. The assignment not only challenged me but fascinated me. In fact, most things outside Cincinnati fascinated me. They showed me a world beyond Ohio was waiting for me if I could find a way out.

After I wrote my paper on Queen Elizabeth II, my perspective on the world changed. I would say to my friends, "I'm going to go to London someday" or "When I graduate, I'm going to see Paris." My friends had such a narrow view of geography, they would say things like "Oh, right. You're going to London, Ohio," or "Paris, Kentucky." Those places did exist, but they weren't the ones I was dying to visit. Sometimes I sat in my class dreaming of what it would be like to go to Europe and see so many of the places I had been reading about.

Eighth grade was a pivotal year not only because it opened my eyes to the world but also because Miss Budke talked to me about having a career. Eighth grade might seem a little early to offer career advice, but she always said it was important for a student to have goals, no matter how old they were. When she asked what I wanted to be when I grew up, I immediately said, "A teacher." She thought that might be a good match for me, and she suggested I think about going to college.

Most kids from my neighborhood didn't go to college. You simply graduated and went to a local business—such as a neighborhood supermarket or restaurant—and got a job. I was surprised she brought up the subject of college at all, let alone to a person who had trouble taking standardized tests. But Miss Budke said she felt that with the right encouragement, I could go far. I told her I had never thought of going to college. She told me to go home, talk to my parents, and see what they thought of the idea.

That night at dinner, I announced, "I'm going to college, and I'm going to become a teacher." My parents stared at me quizzically, so I said it again. More silence. Dad finally said, "You really can't go to college, because we don't have any money. You need a lot of money to go to college."

My dad's impression was that only rich people went to college. He had never known anybody who had gone to college, and neither had Mom, so there was not even any debate on the subject. And I wasn't the only child to think about. At this point, they had three other kids to support. There was no talk about scholarships, because my parents didn't even know financial aid existed.

When I told Miss Budke the bad news, she didn't seem discouraged. She suggested we go to the library to research careers that might not require a college degree. Walking up and down the aisles of the library with her, I came across a book that would change my life. It was called *Cherry Ames, Student Nurse.* What Nancy Drew was to mysteries, Cherry Ames was to the nursing profession. I took it as a good omen that the series was written by a woman named Helen

Wells, because we had the same last name.

I told Miss Budke that although I didn't know very much about medicine, I might like to become a nurse. Aside from my battle with scarlet fever, I very rarely even went to visit the doctor. But the more I thought about it, the more I warmed up to the idea. I could clean a house, do laundry, and cook. I was good at juggling many household tasks at once. That's what I thought nursing probably was. I had no idea about the medical training or expertise it would require.

From the moment I read my first Cherry Ames book, I felt a connection. She took care of people. She bathed people. She made people feel better. I knew I could do all that. I wanted a career that would take me places, and Cherry's role as a nurse took her all over the world. I kept going back to the library until I had read all the Cherry Ames books on the shelf. I devoured *Cherry Ames, Mountaineer Nurse*; *Cherry Ames, Army Nurse*; *Cherry Ames, Island Nurse*, and more. When I was done, I went back and read my favorites again.

The stories in the books and the adventures Cherry had made me definitely want to become a nurse. I just had to keep my grades up and get through high school, so that I could be taken seriously as a candidate for nursing school. Except for Miss Budke, no one encouraged me or guided me. I just had a little dream that becoming a nurse could be my ticket out of Ohio.

CHAPTER THREE

SOMETIMES MOVING TO A new school can open doors, and that's exactly what happened to me after ninth grade, when I graduated from Oyler Junior High. I could have gone to a vocational school, but I chose the college-prep road and went to Western Hills High School, which was also the high school closest to my home. While most of the kids at Oyler were destined to stay in Ohio, many of the students at Western Hills had fathers who were doctors, lawyers, or successful businessmen, and they were clearly going places. It was good timing to arrive at a school with kids like that, because now I had my own game plan, thanks to Miss Budke and the Cherry Ames books.

My friends who didn't go on to Western Hills High either went straight to a vocational school to learn a skill or dropped out of school entirely. I remember one girl—one of my best friends and one of the brightest girls in our class—got pregnant in ninth grade after meeting an older boy who worked in town. They ended up getting married, and she never went back to school. I was devastated for her, because I couldn't imagine my life without the inspiration that school provided. I couldn't fathom the thought of giving up my future at the age of 16 for a boy and a baby.

I worked hard and dedicated myself to taking difficult classes required for nursing school, like Latin and biology. Despite my dreams of nursing school, I was still a pretty typical 1950s teenager. I loved to drink cherry Cokes and roller skate on Friday nights. On Saturdays I helped my mom clean the house, and on Sundays I went with my friends to movie matinees, which cost a quarter. Some Sundays I didn't have a quarter, so I would collect soda pop bottles from the street and turn them in at the neighborhood market. I didn't let on to my fancy school friends that I got my quarter picking up trash in the street.

Movies hypnotized me. They offered a chance to sit in the dark and dream about the lives of other people in faraway places. In fact, I was watching *Wuthering Heights* when I came down with scarlet fever. I could feel my temperature rising, but I didn't want to miss the end of the movie.

Medical melodramas were my favorites. One of the films I liked best was *Magnificent Obsession*, with Rock Hudson and Jane Wyman. In the film, Wyman loses her eyesight in a car accident that Hudson causes, and he becomes a doctor to try and restore it. I loved the movie so much that I saw it two more times.

The movie stars always had such curvy hips, and I envied them—I wore dresses to school, but I would never wear a skirt and a blouse, because I had no hips. I was such a skinny little kid. Sometimes my mother would take me to the doctor and request one of the many tonics that helped kids gain weight. One was called Weight On, and it tasted awful. After nothing worked, the doctor told my mother to ease up on me. He said eventually I would gain weight. And I did. I wasn't exactly curvy, but at least my skirts stayed up.

Dad started every meal with fried potatoes. He would put a skillet on the stove, toss in some lard, and start peeling potatoes. One day, I asked him, "Can't we have something other than potatoes?" And he said, "No. You always have potatoes with your meal." Our dinners included pot roast, pork roast, chili, and other main dishes, but they always came with fried potatoes. We also ate a lot of "mush," which was made from cornmeal. Dad would put a big dab of butter in the center of the bowl and that was dinner. I didn't know until years later that it was unusual to have a dad who cooked dinner in the 1950s.

In the spring and summer, our dinners improved, with an array of fresh tomatoes, green beans, lettuce, and onions, thanks to Dad's vegetable garden. During the summer, Mom would can two or three bushel baskets of apples and peaches. This meant we would have fruit to eat during the winter. Canning and growing our own food was important. You could buy canned goods, ham, and lunchmeat at the supermarket, but they didn't offer a large selection of fruits and vegetables like they do today.

When I wasn't at school, I could usually be found at home babysitting my siblings, Gloria, Jimmy Dale, and Stephen. I secretly thought that my parents didn't have any career aspirations for me because they needed me to take care of the little kids while they went to work.

During the summer, when my high school friends were getting jobs in town, I would have loved to have gotten a job at a dime store, or a movie theater, and learned to run a cash register. But my parents preferred that I stay at home with the little kids. I remember feeling trapped and counting the days until school started again and I could resume my independent routine.

My mom began working again when Stephen was in kindergarten. So now after school, I would clean up the house and start preparing dinner. After dinner, I would do the dishes while my mom started the laundry. Sometimes my dad would stand with me at the sink and dry the dishes so I could get to my homework faster. This continued on the weekends, when I helped my parents clean the house and scrub the floors. Sometimes I would look out the window and see my high school friends playing ball or simply hanging out on the street corner. I remember feeling cheated and hoping there would be more to my life than this.

Even within the walls of our house, I felt different. It was as if I lived in the middle of a strange city, one I didn't belong in. When I watched television shows like *Father Knows Best* and *I Love Lucy*, those families did not resemble ours one bit. As I looked at the faces of the people I lived with, we seemed more like two separate families: There was me and my mom and dad, and there was the family with the four kids who came later.

The older I got, the more out of place I felt, because I had different dreams from my family and friends. During the summer, the Cincinnati Opera often performed at the zoo, an event I first saw when I was in third grade. I was supposed to be looking at the animals with my class, but I couldn't take my eyes off the opera performers. I remember seeing the costumes and hearing the music of

Madame Butterfly and just loving it.

When I played opera music at home, my mom would come in and say, "What is that awful noise?" My family and friends thought I was crazy, but classical music just sounded right to me. I preferred it to the rock-and-roll my friends liked and the loud country music my mother enjoyed. My tastes were simply not the same as theirs. I saw this when I was very young, and the feeling of being different never went away.

My junior year of high school, I joined a sorority called the Sparkettes. I loved being part of such a nice group of young women. I'm in the front row, center.

Being a student at Western Hills High allowed me to meet kids outside my neighborhood crowd. Many of the kids at Western Hills were from middle- to upper-class families. Some of the girls wore cashmere sweaters, Spalding shoes, and real pearls to school. I wanted so much to be like them, I bought imitation pearls and fake brown-and-white Spalding shoes and tried the best I could to fit in. While my neighborhood girlfriends talked about getting married, the girls at Western Hills talked about where they were going to apply to college. I wanted to be as ambitious as they were.

I decided that one way I could become friends with some of the popular girls was to join a sorority, which was basically a girls' social club at school. Some sororities were so popular that you didn't have a prayer of getting into them if you weren't already in one of the popular groups. But I soon learned about a sorority that was easier to get into. It was called the Sparkettes and had been started only six years before I came to Western Hills. I applied and met with some of the girls. It didn't have a Greek name, but it had a solid reputation, and I was thrilled to be accepted into the club.

One of the things I was not thrilled about is that my mother was jealous of the life I was carving out for myself. When I joined the Sparkettes, my mom and dad signed on to be guardians on almost all our field trips. This felt like an invasion of my school time and privacy. I didn't want my parents hanging and hovering around me. I would be with the Sparkettes on a hayride or doing something fun, and there were my mom and dad along for the ride. I knew they had not had a traditional high school experience, but it made me mad that they were butting in on mine.

I looked for ways to set myself apart from my parents. I joined the Future Nurses club, which was a very big deal in those days. During our meetings, we talked about how to get into nursing school and what classes to take in high school. Some of the advisors were doctors' wives. These women were always very well dressed and drove fancy cars. I loved it when the club took a field trip to a hospital, because the doctors' wives would offer to drive us. My favorite doctor's wife had a Buick with a pearl steering wheel. She looked so elegant sitting behind the wheel of that car. I wanted to grow up and be just like her.

Sometimes my friends would invite me for dinner. The wealthier homes had antique furniture, linen napkins, sometimes even live-in maids. Most of these girls had their own bedrooms, which I thought was truly special. One of my best friends in the Sparkettes was a girl named LaDonna. I was amazed that she and her sister, Patty, not only had their own room but that it was upstairs, and their parents' room was downstairs. It almost felt like LaDonna and Patty were living in their own apartment.

During my junior year, I was president of the Sparkettes, president of the Future Nurses club, and president of the Latin club. I felt well connected through my school activities, but sometimes the fact that my parents didn't have much money held me back. For instance, the Latin club took a trip to Washington, D.C. The trip cost $35. My parents didn't have enough to spare, and I couldn't raise the money to travel with the group. I remember feeling so disappointed, especially since I was president of the club, but there was nothing I could do to change the situation.

My activities at school and new circle of friends kept me very busy. Instead of dating individual boys, most of the time we would go out in a group—for instance, on Friday nights to the Western Hills football games. In my senior year, however, I started dating a boy in my class named Jack Schier. After we'd been dating a few months, he gave me the pin from his fraternity, and we started to think beyond graduation. He knew I was not rushing to get married, because I had plans to go to nursing school. Luckily, Jack had plans of his own. He wanted to go into the Navy and then come back to Ohio and study to become a teacher.

I thought Jack and I were a good match, and I was crazy about his parents, an elderly German couple who owned a tailoring shop. Sometimes on Sunday nights, I would eat at his parents' house, where they would serve wonderful dinners of sausages, sauerkraut, and wine they made in their basement. They always had candles and linen napkins on the table. Being around his parents made me feel so continental. Their dinners weren't fancy, but they were the farthest thing from a meal in my parents' house that I could imagine. We rarely sat down to a nice dinner together, because there were so many of us. I much preferred spending time at the Schiers's house, which often bothered my parents.

When I wasn't spending time with Jack, I was with my girlfriends or studying. I didn't want to ruin my chances of getting into nursing school by getting bad grades. I thought it was the beginning of the end when I failed an exam in chemistry. The F stared at me from the page like a big black cloud covering up my future. I knew how important the class was, but I had simply choked on the day of the test.

I mustered all the courage I had and went to talk with my chemistry teacher. I told him that I had studied for the test and knew most of the answers, but that my mind went blank when it came time to put them onto paper. He knew about my goal of getting into nursing school and was very understanding. Fortunately, he agreed to let me retake the test. I went to his classroom one afternoon, and he stood over my shoulder and watched me take the test again. He really was rooting for me. A few times when I put down the wrong answer, he would grunt or groan as a signal for me to reconsider my choice. I finally did pass the test and am eternally grateful to my teacher for letting me retake it.

When I got to Western Hills, I discovered that I didn't want to be the old "me" anymore. I wanted to be the new "me," who fit in with the fancy girls. I knew what I wanted my house to look like. I knew what I wanted to look like. I knew what I wanted my husband and my children to look like. I knew what kind of furniture I wanted and even what kind of sheets I wanted on my bed. At my house, we never had a top sheet, only a bottom sheet and a blanket on top. When I dreamed about the future, there was always a perfectly ironed top sheet on my bed, like the ones I had seen at the fancy houses of my friends at Western Hills.

Seeing those girls with the pearls and the Spalding shoes gave me the incentive to pick up my pace and study harder, so that maybe someday I too could have a lovely family and home. Being with these students who were headed for college made me realize that I didn't have to settle for the hectic, scraping-by-to-make-ends-meet life my parents had arrived at. Getting a good education and becoming a nurse was, I hoped, going to let me have another, better life all my own. But I was faced with a new dilemma as high school ended. I had to find a way to pay for nursing school. Recycling soda pop bottles was not going to be enough.

CHAPTER FOUR

LOOKING BACK, I REALIZE I spent much of my time settling for what I had and stuffing down my emotions. The best example is the Christmas I was 12. In my neighborhood, many kids got one big present, usually something they had asked for. Choosing that gift was something you thought long and hard about; if you got only one present, it had better be good. That year, I said that I wanted a bicycle. My friend Betty Breen, who lived upstairs, asked for one, too. We thought if we had bikes, we could ride together all over the neighborhood. We thought the bikes would make us feel independent and free.

I felt confident in my decision until that November, when I found some kids from our neighborhood snooping around the gardening shed, where my parents stored household items because our apartment was so small. When one of the kids said he had seen a bike in the shed, I announced proudly that it was my Christmas present. Then he told me what kind of bike he had seen. It was not the spiffy red one I had pictured myself cruising the neighborhood on. It was a Donald Duck bike.

When the kids began to tease me, describing how silly I would look on a baby bike, I was devastated. I couldn't bring myself to look inside the shed.

I didn't breathe a word to my parents about it. On Christmas morning, I simply walked into our living room and went straight to a bike sitting near the tree. I feigned surprise; I even went so far as to say that it was exactly what I wanted, and how different and spectacular the yellow-and-blue bike was, with its big Donald Duck head under the handlebars. I knew my parents couldn't return it or afford to buy another one.

Even though Donald's eyes lit up when I rode it and it went "quack, quack" instead of having a bell, I was too proud to let the other kids know how much I disliked it. Betty Breen, of course, got a beautiful burgundy-colored Schwinn. We still rode around the neighborhood together, though it was not the way I had envisioned it. The Donald Duck bike was just one more thing I had to settle for.

My childhood felt hard and uncomfortable. Once I decided to become a nurse, though, I had to look beyond my childhood disappointments and focus on my future.

The most common way of getting an education in the medical field in the 1950s was through a three-year R.N., or Registered Nurse, program. In my senior year, I dedicated myself to researching the nursing programs offered at local hospitals. Some of my teachers helped me, but I did most of the work on my own. Every program cost $100 per year, which covered everything from room and board to uniforms and your first pair of nursing shoes. My parents were so busy, they didn't have an opinion one way or the other. They just wanted me to keep up my chores and babysitting duties.

After visiting four hospitals, I liked Good Samaritan Hospital best. It was where my mother had had all her children except me (because I was born in Hamilton, Ohio). To begin the application process, I had an interview, during which I learned that all those in the program were required to go to chapel each morning. I announced that I wouldn't be able to do that, because I wasn't Catholic. The person interviewing me said I would have to go anyway.

When I went home and contemplated what it would be like to pretend to be Catholic for three years, I decided I couldn't do it. I wanted to become a nurse, not a Catholic. I was looking to embark on a new career, not a new religion. I was a practicing Baptist who went to church every Sunday, and I wasn't about to give that up. And I didn't like the fact that I had to make the choice at all. So I withdrew my application and went in search of a school that would suit me better.

As it turned out, the right program for me was at The Jewish Hospital, which offered everything I was looking for, including a hands-off approach to religion. The hospital was nonsectarian and welcomed nurses of all faiths. Now only one obstacle remained: I didn't have enough money to pay the three years' tuition. I didn't have enough money to pay one year's tuition. I didn't have a job, and my dad was making only $100 a week.

The only paying job I'd ever had was babysitting for other families, which I did on weekends for 50 cents an hour. I would make the kids dinner and get them ready for bed; occasionally I would do some light housecleaning, too, which I didn't mind because the houses were always much nicer than mine. The summer, however, wasn't nearly long enough to earn $100 that way. And my pool of babysitting families dwindled during those months, when many kids went on vacation with their parents or were simply allowed to play outside alone. I had to find some other way to earn my tuition.

I spent a lot of time at my friend LaDonna's house, which made me feel independent. Her mom and dad were older and rarely went upstairs, where LaDonna and her sister had their room. Sometimes my mom would make up things to make me want to come home. She would say, "I'm making your favorite dinner" or something like that. But I didn't want to go home. My mother was pregnant again, and I thought that was strange. My friends' parents were all done having children, and I thought my mother should be done, too.

Every summer, LaDonna and her sister and mother worked at Camp Sunshine, somewhere in northern Kentucky. LaDonna was a counselor; Patty, a junior counselor; and their mother, the camp cook. Their father would drive back and forth on weekends. When LaDonna said the camp might need extra help, I asked her parents if I could go to Camp Sunshine with them, and they said yes. My parents seemed fine with the idea, but I remember thinking they were in complete denial that one day I would be leaving home for good.

My high school graduation ceremony was held in June 1957 in the Cincinnati Music Hall. That marked a significant educational milestone in our family. My mother had dropped out of school after eighth grade, and my dad never got past third grade. As the first in my family to graduate from high school, I felt very proud. My parents were not the most affectionate people, with each other or their children. I saw how other parents hugged, kissed, and doted on their children, and it felt very different in my house, where there was no hugging at all. Even so, though they didn't always know how to show it, I know my parents felt proud, too.

After the ceremony, we had a party at LaDonna's house and stayed up all night. LaDonna was going to college in Kentucky. Betty was going into the U.S. Air Force. Some of my other friends were getting jobs; one girl even got married that night. We were all heading in different directions.

Jack was getting ready to leave for Detroit to enlist in the Navy. That night, he gave me his class ring. He said it meant that even though we were going to be apart, we were still a couple. I liked the sound of that, so I accepted the ring. He said he would try to come home for the holidays, and we could look forward to that.

The next morning, we had a picnic breakfast in the park and shared our plans for the summer. I was so happy to be headed to Camp Sunshine. I had never been to a sleep-away camp, but I was eager to go. In addition to being a counselor, I would work in the kitchen. LaDonna's mother had said my job would be washing dishes, which happened to be a task at which I was quite proficient. When I told her that I needed $100

In 1957, I worked as a counselor at Camp Sunshine. The money I earned helped me pay my tuition at nursing school.

for my first year of nursing school, she thought that would be fair payment. Looking back, it seems a small amount to be paid for an entire summer's work, but I was happy, because it was what I needed.

Camp Sunshine was for underprivileged kids who lived in the urban ghettos of Cincinnati. The camp had modified tent-cabins, a big recreation hall with a kitchen, and a beautiful swimming pool. As a counselor, I had one immediate flaw that I was unable to hide: I didn't know how to swim. I did own a swimsuit, because I'd gone regularly to a pool across the street from my high school. All my friends and I ever did there was work on our tans and paddle around in the shallow end, waiting for boys to talk to us.

So there I was, my first time at a sporty summer camp, and I had no idea how to swim. I could dogpaddle well enough to stay afloat, but that was about it. My first week there, though, the swimming counselor put me on the spot in front of all the campers; I literally had to sink or swim. I not only learned to swim that summer, I also had a great time.

The week after I came home, my mother gave birth to her final child, Brenda. When she called to tell us the news, she said, "Bring your $100 from camp. I need it."

"No!" I said. "I need it to pay for nursing school."

"I'll pay you back in time. But your dad's insurance check didn't arrive, and I need $100 to get me and the baby out of the hospital."

I had no choice but to give her my $100. The timing could not have been more coincidental, like a lot of things in my life. I had just earned $100 and my mother was in desperate need of the exact same amount.

We waited and waited for the insurance check to arrive. In those days, we had morning and afternoon mail delivery. Every day, twice a day, I would run up the driveway to look for the check. And wouldn't you know it: The check arrived the day I left for nursing school. Just in time.

When I left home for The Jewish Hospital, I was 18 years old. Jimmy was 11; Gloria, 8; Stephen, 7; and Brenda, just a few weeks old. It was hard to say goodbye to them, because I had practically raised the three older kids and would not get a chance to really know Brenda until much later in our lives. But it was important for them to learn to rely on our mother, and for me to leave. When it was time to say goodbye to my brothers and sisters, I gave each of them a big hug.

I had packed my small blue Samsonite overnight bag with my nightgown, cosmetics, and a few essentials, because my dad had said, "I don't think you'll be there that long. Just take an overnight bag." It wasn't that he wanted me to fail. Rather, it was just inconceivable to him that I would move out of the home I'd lived in for 18 years. As I got on the first of the two buses that would take me to The Jewish Hospital School of Nursing, I knew I would return for the rest of my clothes. I would miss my parents, but I was never moving back.

CHAPTER FIVE

I HAD SPENT SO many years sharing a cluttered, overcrowded room with my brothers and sisters that I couldn't wait to have a room to call my own. I used to sit on my bunk bed at night and dream about what it would look like. At the nursing school, my room had two beds, two desks, two dressers, two bookshelves, and two closets. Many might have called the room plain, but I thought it was the most beautiful room in the world, because I only had to share it with one person.

My roommate, Maureen, and I had met in the Future Nurses club at Western Hills High. When we got our acceptance letters to The Jewish Hospital, we decided to room together, though we didn't know each other very well.

I especially liked that we each had our own bookshelf. A whole shelf just for my books!

I also liked that we each had a new bedspread. When I pulled mine down for the first time, I saw the bed had both top and bottom sheets. The only time I had ever slept with a top sheet was when I spent the night at LaDonna's house. I thought it was so grand not to feel the scratchy blanket against my skin. That first night at the nursing school, I slept the soundest sleep I'd had in months.

Our room was in a dorm called Greenwood Hall, a beautiful old building connected to the hospital by a tunnel. When we left to go to the hospital, we never had to put our coats on. There were six floors, and the graduate nurses lived on the top floor. We made our own beds, but the housekeepers assigned to each floor dusted the furniture, swept the floors, and cleaned the communal bathrooms. The bathroom on each floor had four stall showers and six toilets and sinks. Each floor also had a little kitchenette. Though we ate most of our meals in the hospital cafeteria, we sometimes grabbed a peanut-butter-and-jelly sandwich from the refrigerator. Everything was organized so that all we had to do was concentrate on studying to become nurses. Even our classrooms were in the basement of that building.

The dorm had a gymnasium that served double duty, as a basketball court and a stage for the variety shows we put on. There were two payphones on each floor, and each floor had a television. When we had time, we would watch our favorite shows. We all liked *I Love Lucy* and *The Ed Sullivan Show*.

Our pride in being student nurses showed in the way we took care of our uniforms: a short-sleeved pink dress that buttoned in the front, with an apron and white collar and cuffs. The dress and apron would go to the school laundry, but we had to clean and starch our collars and cuffs ourselves. I made a little extra money by cleaning other girls' collars and cuffs for 50 cents. I would wash them, soak them in liquid starch, then hang them across a mirror to dry. After you tied the collar around your neck, you'd fasten it to your bra with a shoelace so that it would stand up straight.

A housemother kept track of our comings and goings. On weeknights, we were supposed to be in bed at 10 p.m., and we were not allowed to receive any more phone calls until morning. If one of the girls was making noise or listening to music, the housemother would come knocking on her door. During the week, we stayed in the dorm to study, do laundry, and wash out our nursing collars and cuffs. On weekends, we had a later curfew.

The first six months of nursing school, which took place entirely in the classroom, was considered a probation period. They even called us "probies," to remind us that we were being watched closely. We had heard from upperclassmen that if we could survive it, we were probably going to graduate, because the first six months of the three-year program were considered the most difficult. Previous first-year classes, we heard, had lost half their classmates after the probation period. I worried that I might become one of the girls to go home early. I didn't know what I would do if I lost my chance of becoming a nurse.

After almost failing chemistry in high school, it was an incredible relief to pass that class, but I began to struggle in several others. Microbiology was particularly difficult for me. When I got a call to meet privately with my microbiology teacher, I made my way to her office preparing for the worst.

She was sitting at her desk with my workbook open in front of her. I looked down at the book, and she showed me my score. It was below a D. I stared at the grade and began to cry. I thought she was telling me that it was time to pack my bags.

"What are we going to do about this?" she asked sternly.

I knew things looked bad, but I wasn't ready to give up nursing just yet.

"I don't know what you are going to do, but I'm not leaving," I said.

I think she understood that I was serious. It was pretty obvious that I was not cut out to be a groundbreaking microbiologist, but I had the potential to become a good nursing candidate. She started going through my workbook, reevaluating what I'd done and adding a point here and there. When she got the number up to 72 so that I could get a C, I was never so happy in my life. I told her I wouldn't let her down. I would work harder, study more, and show her that I could improve.

My roommate, Maureen, turned out to be very quiet and shy. She never wanted to meet new people, while I was eager to make as many friends as possible, and I made many new girlfriends that year. My core friends included Freda, Wilma, Sondra, Phyllis, and Sue, who were all from Kentucky or Ohio. I also met some nice upper classmates, including Norma Kaye from Cincinnati, whose mother was a nurse at The Jewish Hospital.

I was surprised to find that some girls in my class were poorer than I was. About a third were from wealthy families, and many of them didn't make it through the probation period. The rich girls could sometimes be prima donnas, thinking they shouldn't have to do grunt work like cleaning bedpans. The poorer girls like me thought hard work came with the territory.

When the six-month probation period was over, I was so relieved when I made the cut. Nearly all my friends on my floor were able to come back, too. The school had assigned each of us a "big sister," and mine was a senior named Millee. We heard a rumor that she had suffered a nervous breakdown—the school said she left because of "health issues"—and we never heard from her again.

But my friends and I were ready to shed our probie label and move on with our studies. The next step was to hone our nursing skills in a ward set up in the basement of our dormitory. It had 20 beds and all the medical equipment you might find on a typical hospital floor—everything but patients, which we would get to later. We also had classes in lab rooms now, as well as lectures in other classrooms.

During the probie period, we had had some weekends free, but that was the last time our weekends would be our own. Now we spent our weekends on the floor of the real hospital. Nursing students earned $7 for an eight-hour shift. If we worked both Saturday and Sunday, we would get $7 in cash for one of the days and a school credit for the other day. Monday through Friday, we either attended classes or picked up extra shifts in the hospital, working from 3 to 10 p.m.

The academic classes continued to be difficult for me; I felt we were being tested all the time. I enjoyed classes such as Nursing Arts, where we learned hands-on aspects of care: how to take someone's temperature, how to take a blood-pressure reading. We learned how to give injections by inserting a needle into the tough skin of an orange. It took a lot of practice; we went through dozens of oranges until we could give a shot with ease.

Making a hospital bed was like nothing I had ever seen done before. There were no such things as fitted sheets, so you had to contour the sheets to fit the bed just right. And you couldn't run around the bed to complete the task, either. You always had to pretend a patient was lying in the middle. You made up one side, then rolled the imaginary patient onto his side and pulled the sheets out from underneath him. Then you made up the other side of the bed.

If the head nurse didn't think you'd done a perfect job, you had to do it all over again.

At first, we never dealt with seriously ill patients. We were assigned patients who were taking tests or recuperating from non-life-threatening surgery. In those days, if you had an appendectomy, you stayed in the hospital for a week. If you had a baby, you remained for at least ten days. There were plenty of patients who were in need of care but were not medically fragile.

There was one instructor for every six student nurses. The instructor would follow us around and make sure we were adhering to proper procedure. She would also grade us on such things as personality: how we talked to a patient, what we said to a doctor, how we interacted with other nurses on the floor. We were even graded on how we cleaned up the room after a patient was discharged. It seemed like we were graded on absolutely everything.

One day when I was working on the floor, I noticed that the head nurse gave five-minute breaks to the students who smoked cigarettes or drank coffee. She would say, "Jane and Sarah, go and take your break. And Barbara, you cover the next two patients." I couldn't believe the preferential treatment that smokers were given. I didn't smoke or drink coffee, but in that first year of nursing school, I picked up both habits. If other girls were getting breaks, I wanted to take them, too. I asked a few of the girls on my floor to teach me how to smoke, and soon nicotine and caffeine were part of my daily routine. Before I knew it, the head nurse was giving me five-minute breaks.

I spent so much time studying or working at the hospital, it left little time to visit my parents. I made it home about once a month and for holidays like Thanksgiving and Christmas. Sometimes when the other girls went home, however, I stayed in the dorm. I liked it because it was quiet and gave me a chance to study on my own. I spent some of my free time playing on the nursing school's various sports teams; I was on the volleyball team and even earned a letter. We played our games in the dorm's gymnasium, where dances were held occasionally.

In those days, no males were allowed in the nursing school, so the only place to meet boys our age was the mortuary school. It was just down the street from our dorm—if you stood in the middle of the street, you could see it. While we were learning how to give injections to oranges, they were at the city morgue learning how to embalm bodies. They came to our dances about once a month.

With a few of my friends—Nancy, Betty, and Marge—I started spending time with some of the mortuary students on weekends. Sometimes we would go to one guy's apartment, and the girls and I would clean it, buy food, and make them dinner. But most weekend nights, they had to work at the morgue, so we would tag along. Lying on slabs there were mostly unclaimed bodies, or "John Does," and those were the bodies on which they practiced embalming.

As much as they wanted to become morticians and funeral directors, these guys also had a penchant for poker. Many times, after they set up a poker game, Nancy, Betty, Marge, and I would finish the embalming. By then, they would have taken the organs out of the bodies and placed them in formaldehyde. Our job was to dust the organs, put them back in the body, and sew it up. The funny thing was, you didn't have to put all the organs in the proper location. They just had to fit into the body they had come from. Sometimes we couldn't get a brain back in without lifting up the scalp. But nothing about the process really bothered us.

These were just fun guys to hang out with. Nobody took it too seriously, particularly me, since I was still involved with Jack. I stayed in touch with his parents, too. When I was home, I often went to their house for dinner. In fact, sometimes I would spend the whole weekend with them and sleep in Jack's room.

After he finished his basic training, in Detroit, Jack planned to go to California for his longer assignment with the Navy. Despite the long-distance relationship, we remained crazy about each other. We wrote letters all the time, because we could not afford to make long-distance phone calls. I was a big letter writer back then. I wrote letters to nearly everyone I knew, including my high school friends who had stayed home and gotten jobs. I always kept stationery and stamps in a box by my bed. I probably wrote ten letters a week.

When I was with Jack again at Thanksgiving, it was as if we had never been apart. We got along so well, we even started talking about a future together. Even so, I gave him back his class ring. I was quite practical about it. I said, "It is silly for us to pretend we are a couple when we are so far away from each other. You might meet someone, and I might meet someone." I felt we really didn't know what would happen. I had two and a half years of nursing school left, and I needed to focus on that. He took the ring back, and we said goodbye for now.

The months seemed to fly by, and when spring rolled around, I was faced with a new problem: How was I going to pay the tuition for my second and third years? I worked part-time in the hospital for $7 a shift, and I babysat for some of the doctors, but I didn't make anywhere near enough money for that. And besides, now I had other expenses, such as cigarettes and stockings. I asked around for advice, and one of my teachers suggested that I write to the hospital board.

Although I loved corresponding with my friends and family, I was not used to writing formal business letters. But I had nothing to lose. I told the board members that I was very happy at school, that I loved nursing, and that, though I wasn't a straight-A student, I thought I was doing well. I had gotten very good reviews of my work. I told them how much I wanted to stay in school but that I didn't have the money to pay the next year's tuition.

My letter was probably filled with misspelled words, but it said what I wanted it to say. When I asked the girls on my end of the floor to read it, though, many just laughed. One said, "Who cares? The board is not going to help you. They don't even know you. You'd better think of someplace else to get the money."

I always try to remain optimistic. I decided to send the letter anyway, hoping the board members would understand and find a way to help me. I didn't know where else to get the money. And if I couldn't become a nurse, I didn't know what I would do with my life.

A week or two later, I got a letter from the hospital board. It said how happy they were that I was doing so well, and they wanted me to stay. They promised to cover the fee for not only my second year but my third year as well. The $200 would come from a scholarship fund I had never heard of—people didn't talk much about scholarships in those days. Financially, I would be set until graduation.

I told my parents the good news, but they didn't take my dreams seriously. They still thought I would eventually move back home. That, of course, was not my plan at all.

CHAPTER SIX

MAUREEN WAS AN ONLY child. There was a rumor that her dad had died at Pearl Harbor, but we never talked about his death, or the rest of her family, for that matter. We didn't talk about much of anything, because she was so very shy. And as I said, she never wanted to make any friends. Because we were so different, it didn't come as a surprise to either of us that in our second year, we chose not to room together.

When I asked our housemother if I could have another room, she said she had a single available. It was much nicer than the room I'd shared with Maureen. It came with a big dresser and a bathroom that I shared with a girl named Leisla. And it was nice making a new friend.

Just as the school year began, I became a patient myself, so I got to see what things were like from the other side of the bed. Throughout most of my childhood, I had suffered from sore throats. We never did much about them, because, although my dad's job paid for medical insurance, it covered hospitalization, not doctor's visits. The solution for most everything then was to take aspirin. In nursing school, however, we got free medical care. When I got a sore throat, a doctor told me my tonsils were infected and I should have them taken out.

I checked into the hospital in the afternoon and had my surgery early the next morning. It was such routine surgery that I didn't even ask my parents to come. However, something strange happened: The nursing staff forgot about me. When no one brought me any lunch or dinner, I began to wonder what was going on. Our hospital did not have a pediatrics ward, only a few surgical beds for children having their tonsils removed. Since all the children had been discharged, I guess I just fell through the cracks. Finally, I called some of my girlfriends in the dorm and asked them to help me check out. I can't say I was impressed with the care I received. My stay in the hospital motivated me to become a better nurse.

One of the biggest things we learned was how to be organized and prioritize our steps. Everything had to be plotted out methodically and put on a schedule. When you had a list of patients to deal with, you planned their day from morning until late afternoon, when your shift ended. You had to easily access what each patient would need. We would go through the linen closet and select the linens they'd use. We would go to the supply closet to collect everything needed for treatment, especially for changing bandages.

During our second year, we rotated among various disciplines—for instance, in the surgical ward, obstetrics, and recovery—spending three months focused on each. Since there was no pediatrics ward, we did that rotation in a nearby children's hospital; during those three months, we lived in its dorms. One of the most interesting

1958, my first year of nursing school. I felt so proud to be wearing my cap.

In 1958, I went with a group of young nursing students to Atlantic City.

rotations was at a tuberculosis hospital. There, we worked alongside girls from nursing schools in other cities. In each hospital, the nurses wore a different style cap. The nurses from Boston had gorgeous fluted caps. Because of our work, we felt an instant camaraderie, but our caps differentiated us.

In addition to our floor rotations, we learned about the procedures used in a pharmacy. We had to memorize lists of medications and what their benefits and side effects were. While there weren't as many medications then, we were required to learn about the most frequently used drugs, such as insulin, sulfa, and penicillin. One day, an FBI officer taught us about illegal substances. He brought in some marijuana to show us what it looked like. He even lit up a joint so we would be able to recognize the smell. He told us to call the police if we ever suspected a patient had been using illegal drugs.

I was very impressionable back then. Everything was new to me, and with each rotation, I found myself smitten with that specialty. One day I wanted to be a pediatric nurse; the next day I wanted to work in surgery. Everything seemed so interesting that I wasn't sure how I was ever going to decide what kind of nurse I wanted to be.

I had a friend, Donna Palmer, who had already graduated and lived on the top floor of the dorm. She was in charge of three beds in the medical unit on the third floor of the hospital, which is where I worked. She would stop by the nursing station to do her charts, and that's how I got to know her.

Donna was from Batesville, Indiana, and like me, she had been ready to escape the Midwest for a long time. I would sometimes go home with her on weekends. I knew she was never going to move back to Indiana. Like me, she had too many siblings living in an overcrowded house—definitely not the kind of situation you would run home to—and her family was even poorer than mine. And she was a girl with a lot of potential. It didn't hurt that she was one of the prettiest nurses in the entire dorm.

Donna worked at a research institute where they were studying the possibility of kidney transplants. That seems routine today, but it was unheard of in the 1950s. The research entailed taking the kidneys of newborns who had died and trying to implant them in sick adults. Donna got to know her kidney patients very well, but unfortunately, most of them died.

Donna let me shadow her on a day the doctors were making their first attempt at dialysis. Today, of course, sophisticated equipment speeds up the process, and it is far more comfortable. Back then, the procedure was extremely time consuming and labor intensive. Donna showed me a big tub filled with water and plastic tubing, where a woman was going to be attached to the equipment for 24 hours. Being around every aspect of a field from research to surgery to innovation was fascinating. I wondered if this type of research would be a good fit for me.

One night, I was working in the newborn nursery, taking care of a baby in an incubator. He was having difficulty breathing, and the family had already given the doctors in Donna's research institute permission to harvest his kidneys after he died. It looked as if he would not make it to the morning. The only thing I had on hand was a caffeine stimulant, and through the night, I injected the baby with it. In the morning, when the doctors found him doing well, they were really surprised. I saved the baby but ruined a transplant opportunity. Eventually, he went home and was able to breath on his own.

My head was down in my books for most of that fall, but Jack brought me up for air while I was doing my rotation at the children's hospital. Though I had given him back his class ring, we still wrote constantly. He was based in California now, and when he came home that December, I was desperate to be with him. I outlined a plan to convince my head nurse to give me more time off.

We got two days off each week, and I wanted six. I figured if I worked really hard, I could ask to take my two days off plus two extra days the following week. I asked for Christmas and the day after Christmas; in exchange, I would work New Year's Eve and New Year's Day. Most of my friends told me not to bother. They said head nurses never cared about boyfriend stories. They were a dime a dozen.

I thought I could make a better case if I wrote my request in a letter. That way, I could avoid sounding silly or emotional. I explained why I was asking for the time off and what I was willing to do to make it up. And sure enough, when the schedule came out the following week, I had my six consecutive days off! I was so excited to have so much time to spend with Jack. I couldn't wait.

We met at his parents' house and had a lovely Christmas week. Jack's gift was a stuffed cat wearing a red suit and a full-size strand of pearls. I didn't have any nice jewelry, and I thought it was the most beautiful necklace I had ever seen. It reminded me of the ones the wealthy girls at Western Hills High wore to dances with their cashmere sweater sets. I couldn't believe I had a pearl necklace of my very own.

We talked about marriage that Christmas. It seemed the natural thing to do, because we were so much in love, and we felt we had our career paths planned out. We talked to his parents, and we spoke with my parents. Everybody got along well, and before we knew it, we were all planning a big wedding. I liked the idea of the wedding because it would help keep me occupied while Jack was away.

After Christmas, he flew back to California, where he would be stationed for the next year. A few months later, a ring with a single small diamond came in the mail, with a letter from Jack asking me to marry him. I was officially engaged. In a room full of student nurses, my friend Freda got down on one knee, read the letter aloud, and placed the ring on my finger. I couldn't believe it was sitting right on my ring finger like that. My friends immediately began helping me plan my wedding. Meanwhile, Jack and I wrote letters back and forth almost every day.

We decided I would have six bridesmaids, all friends from nursing school. We picked a date, April 16, in the spring of my third and final year of nursing school. I selected a long white wedding dress, put it on layaway, and began paying it off at $10 a month. During the next few months, we made decisions about the bridesmaids' dresses, the invitations, the church, the refreshments (tea and cookies), and the wedding cake at the reception. I would be the first of my nursing friends to get married, and I think that's one of the reasons all the girls were excited to be planning my wedding.

With Jack gone, I had fewer distractions and more time to dedicate to my studies. At night, most of the girls would play bridge or canasta or listen to loud music, but I always had to study to keep up my grades. Between the card games and the music, it was sometimes difficult to concentrate. Then I noticed a broom closet at the end of my hall. There were lots of brooms stored inside, but it had a light. I climbed in with my books, shut the door behind me, and turned on the light. It proved to be the perfect place to study.

One day, we learned we had a new director of nursing, named Helen Rigdon. She brought us all into the gymnasium and told us that she intended to have an open-door policy. This meant that if someone had a problem, small or big, we should feel free to come to her, and she would try to help us. Compared with our teachers, she seemed very approachable, and we liked her right away.

I told Freda how impressed I was that Rigdon had said to go to her with our problems. That's when Freda confided that she had a problem. She was pregnant. The father of the baby worked at a nearby psychiatric hospital, and she didn't know him very well. They had only been on a few dates. I knew that some of my fellow students were experimenting with sex, though there was little talk of birth control. I didn't know how to advise Freda, so with her permission I went to see Rigdon.

This news presented Rigdon with a dilemma: As much as she wanted to help her, Rigdon was afraid if she didn't expel Freda, it would put her job in jeopardy. People already viewed her as an outsider, because she was new; she had been at The Jewish Hospital just a few weeks. We knew some of the older teachers were waiting for her to trip up so they could get her fired. But Rigdon decided to be a maverick and save Freda's nursing career instead of expelling her.

The next day, I took Freda to Rigdon's apartment. It was to the advantage of both for Freda to deal with her pregnancy away from the school. We decided we would tell the other student nurses that she had gone home to help her mother, who was about to have a baby. This was true and completely believable; her mother was in her forties and could no doubt use some help with an infant. Freda would live with a friend of Rigdon's in Michigan, an OB-GYN, until she gave birth to her own baby and put it up for adoption. After that, we hoped, she could resume her studies to become a nurse, and she did.

To set the plan in motion, Rigdon sent me to Kentucky to talk with Freda's parents. I had met them, and she thought it would be best if I talked to them face to face. They were not very sophisticated, almost unable to understand what I was saying. When I told them their daughter was pregnant, her father said, "Can we claim this child on our income taxes?"

It was frustrating to think they cared more about money than their daughter's future. After a lengthy discussion, however, they finally understood the situation, and that it was best to keep this pregnancy a secret. They understood that if anyone from the school administration called, they should say their daughter was with them to help with their new baby.

The following week, Rigdon took Freda to the train station at 4 a.m. and sent her off to Michigan. A few months later, Rigdon asked me if I would like to visit Freda before the baby was born. I said yes, I would. I was with Freda in the pre-admitting department of the hospital while an intake nurse was asking for information.

"Father's name," she inquired.

"None," mumbled Freda.

"Oh, you're the girl who has been living with the doctor and his wife. I heard about you," said the nurse condescendingly. I had never felt so sorry for anyone.

Freda delivered a healthy baby and then gave him up for adoption, to a doctor and his wife in St. Louis. The nurses never let her hold her baby or even see him. They only told her she'd had a baby boy. She returned to nursing school the following year and carried on as if nothing had happened. As far as I know, only Rigdon and I knew the truth. I'll never forget how hard this was for Freda, or how nice it was of Rigdon to help her. I don't know what would have happened to Freda if we hadn't been there. She was able to graduate from nursing school, and later she married and had three more children.

I had known girls in my high school who had gotten pregnant and dropped out, but this affected me more. To get pregnant in nursing school was to put not only your medical career but your entire future in jeopardy. I couldn't imagine anything more frightening. I had just one more year to go before I became a nurse, and I wasn't going to let anything or anyone stand in my way.

CHAPTER SEVEN

MY THIRD YEAR OF nursing school became all about planning my wedding. When we weren't preparing for the wedding, we sat around talking about the wedding, or about what life would be like once I was married. My friends had already ordered name tags for my uniform that read "Mrs. Barbara Schier." In those days, there were no iron-on name tags, so I had to sew each one on individually.

I remember thinking that life was going to be so wonderful. In April, I would be getting married. In June, I would graduate from nursing school. By that fall, I would be a happily married woman working in a hospital and wearing my new name tags.

My friends threw a few bridal showers and parties for me, but Jack couldn't attend any of them, because he wasn't scheduled to leave the Navy until the week before the wedding. I wrote him a letter every day and told him about the presents pouring in. He had a lot of aunts, uncles, and cousins whom I had never met, and I told him the names on the gift cards but promised I wouldn't open any of the gifts until he was back in Cincinnati. My mother put all the beautifully wrapped boxes in her living room. Some were stacked so high, they reached the ceiling.

Occasionally, the student nurses would put on a weekend variety show in the gymnasium, and that's what we were preparing the week before my wedding. I had a part in a comedy scene that required wearing thick, oil-based stage makeup. The girls knew that Jack was arriving that Saturday night, so instead of acting onstage in all that makeup that night, I was put in charge of pulling the curtain.

I worked my last night at the hospital from Thursday at 11 p.m. until Friday at 7 a.m. It was very quiet on the floor, but I had a medical aide with me in case things got busy. Medical aides moved around the hospital, providing extra support where needed; we referred to them as floaters. The floater with me that night was an

African American woman I had never met before.

Around 3 a.m., we had nothing to do, and we struck up a conversation.

"What are you doing this weekend?" she asked me.

"My fiancé is coming home from California," I said. "We're getting married next weekend."

"What is he doing in California?" she asked.

"He's finishing up in the Navy before coming back here to go to college." I was so proud and excited about our plans.

"What will you do if he doesn't come home?" she asked.

I thought it was the strangest question I had ever heard.

"What do you mean? Of course he is coming home. We're getting married."

"I know, but strange things happen sometimes, and you should be prepared for anything," she cautioned.

"Well, it'd better not happen, because I have to pick up my wedding dress. It's all paid for," I said.

"But if he didn't come home—I mean, really didn't come back—what would you do?" she persisted.

Realizing she wanted an honest answer, I thought for a minute. "I would finish school and become a nurse, just like I planned," I said.

"I'm glad you are looking at all the angles," she said.

Jack was taking a flight from Los Angeles to Cincinnati and was due in that Saturday at 9 p.m. The airport was so small then, and there were so few flights, it didn't take long to meet someone who had just flown in. He would call when his plane landed, and my mom and I would rush to the airport.

My suitcases were packed and sitting in my dorm room waiting for me. We planned to honeymoon in Florida, where Jack's brother, a teacher, and his wife lived. Jack, of course, often talked about becoming a teacher himself. I had never been to Florida and was thrilled when his brother offered to buy us round-trip tickets for a two-week honeymoon. Everything was ready; all I had to do was sit back and wait for Jack.

The variety show went on at 8 p.m., and my mom sat backstage with me. The gymnasium was just off the main lobby of my dorm. In the lobby, a receptionist took phone calls at an old-fashioned plug-in phone board. She knew to send someone to get me as soon as Jack's call came in. Shortly after 9 p.m., one of my friends came running backstage and said, "Quick, quick, Barbara, Jack's on the phone. Go to Rigdon's office so you can talk in private."

I picked up the phone in Rigdon's office and said, "Hi. Where are you? You're a little bit late. Was your plane delayed?"

There was silence on the other end of the line.

"Jack? Are you there? Was your plane late?" I said.

"No," he said. "The plane was not late. I'm still in California."

"What do you mean you're still in California? Did they cancel your flight?"

"Barbara...."

"You're supposed to be here. Mom is here. I'm waiting for you. I'm all packed."

"There's been a problem." He paused. "I'm not coming home right now."

"What are you talking about?" I said, stunned. "We're getting married in a week."

"There's been an accident at the base, an explosion. Some sailors have been killed. Everyone's leave has been canceled," Jack said. "I can't come home until they sort out what happened. I think we're going to have to postpone the wedding."

"But our wedding is on Saturday," I said, a fact he already knew. "Can't you tell whoever is in charge that you need to come home? I'm sorry about the accident, but what about the wedding?"

"I think we're going to have to postpone the wedding," he repeated.

Just then, my mom walked into Rigdon's office, and she could tell I was upset.

"What's going on?" she said. "What's the problem?"

"There's been an accident, and Jack didn't get on the plane. He's not coming home."

I started to feel dizzy, so I quickly sat down. My mom grabbed the phone.

"Let me talk some sense into him," she said, bossy as always.

He told her the same story.

"Well, call us tomorrow," she said, and she hung up. I got up in a daze, and as we left Rigdon's office, I started to cry. We walked down the hall just as people were coming out of the auditorium after the show. My mother guided me up to my dorm room, where we picked up my suitcases. I was in a fog as we got into the elevator, tears streaming down my face. As the elevator doors closed, I could hear some of my friends saying, "What's happening?" "What's wrong with Barbara?" "Why is she crying?"

When I got to my mother's house, we didn't talk about Jack or the wedding. I climbed into bed and immediately went to sleep.

The next morning, Mom suggested we go see Jack's parents and start making arrangements to postpone the wedding. We were now just six days from the ceremony, and in the days before faxes or emails, we had a lot of work to do to notify all the wedding guests. We decided to call the minister at Pricehill Baptist Church and let him know, and then put an ad in the newspaper for everyone to read.

Before we left the house, we got a phone call. To be specific, my dad got a phone call, which was odd, because my dad never got phone calls. As he moved to take the call, my mom grabbed the phone.

"Talk to me," she said. "I'm his wife."

The man on the other end insisted on speaking to Dad. Reluctantly, Mom handed the phone to him, and he waved us out of the kitchen. Mom and I walked outside to discuss the newspaper ad. A few minutes later, Dad came outside, too.

"Well, that was the chaplain from the Navy base in California. He told me the real story about what happened to Jack."

"Real story?" I said. "Dad, what are you talking about?"

Then my dad, slowly but steadily, began to tell the hardest story he would ever have to tell anyone. Jack had been at the airport, preparing to board the plane, the chaplain told him, when he was arrested by a couple of military-police officers. Apparently, he had been dating the daughter of a Navy officer. I was not the only woman in his life—and they were going to have a baby. Jack had been attempting to run away from his problems there by coming home to marry me.

Despite feeling incredibly sad and terribly betrayed, I remember feeling fortunate that I'd found out the truth in time. The situation certainly could have been worse, if I had married Jack before I found out about his pregnant girlfriend.

When my dad finished talking, he started to cry, and so did I. Then Mom started crying, too. We took a few moments to let it all sink in, and then we pulled ourselves together. The reality was that we had to get to work and let all the guests know, via the newspaper ad and other avenues, that the wedding was not just postponed, it was canceled.

But first, we had to go to Jack's parents and tell them the truth. My relationship with Jack was over. We were not getting married in six days or six months. My mom and I took the bus downtown to the tailoring shop where Jack's parents worked. Though it was Sunday, we knew they would be there.

When we walked into their shop, we could see from the look on Mr. Schier's face that he already knew. The chaplain at the Navy base had called him, too. However, he had not told his wife yet. She started saying how all we had to do was postpone the wedding for a few weeks, how everything was going to be fine. After a few minutes, I couldn't stand it anymore, and I blurted out the truth. We all watched as Jack's mother painfully absorbed the news. It was difficult to see, but the facts needed to be said out loud.

His mother was humiliated by the news and overwhelmed with grief. Suddenly, she threatened to go down to the nearest bridge and jump. It was 1960, and people didn't get girls pregnant and cancel weddings every day. It was a terrible embarrassment for Jack's family. I did the only thing I could think of: I gave Mr. and Mrs. Schier each a hug and told them everything would be okay. We would all get on with our lives.

Then my mom and I walked out the door, and we never saw them again. It felt strange, because we had grown very close. Over the last two years, I had eaten many dinners with them, even slept in their house. But we knew that Jack's actions had consequences, and they would change our lives. We could not pretend to be family, or even friends.

When we got back to my dorm, we called Jack's brother. We told him to fly to Cincinnati as soon as he could to be with his parents; we were afraid they might both jump off a bridge. Then we sat down with Miss Rigdon and told her the whole story.

The three of us decided that I still should take off the two weeks I had planned for our honeymoon. It would give me time to think and to rest. I didn't feel I had the emotional strength to tell my friends about my problem, so Rigdon said she would do that. She also had a suggestion.

"Barbara, I think you should go into my office and call Jack. I'm sure you can get him on the phone; he must be confined to quarters. You can ask for the chaplain, and the chaplain can get him. He probably thinks you still believe the story about the explosion. I think you need to tell him you know the truth. And you do need to speak to him in person rather than by letter," she added matter-of-factly, "so you can finalize everything." She had always given good advice, so I followed her lead in this, too.

When I think back, it seems like it was a dream rather than something that happened to me. I suppose I was just going through the motions, without feeling much or giving things much thought. I remember talking to Jack and saying, "The chaplain called our fathers, and we all know the truth. I want you to know that I know you will be fine. And I will be fine, too. Things happen in life that we are not always prepared for. I think we both will get over this, and I hope you have a happy life."

There was no yelling or screaming from either of us. He told me that he was sorry, that he felt bad about it all. When I asked what he wanted me to do with the engagement ring, he told me to keep it. He didn't want it back. Then we said goodbye.

When I got home, I looked at my mom and said, "What am I going to do now?" The unopened presents were in piles all around me, reminders of the wedding that would never take place.

My mother suggested that I get on a train and go to visit my grandmother in Tulsa. I couldn't think of another plan. When I got to Tulsa, I told my grandmother the whole story, and she was very sympathetic. Over the next two weeks, we visited relatives across the state and spent a lot of time with my Aunt Johnny and her son Donald, who was close to my age. Every time I told my story to someone, it got easier. It felt less painful. Soon, it was as if I were telling a story about another girl, someone I knew as a friend.

While I was at my grandmother's house, I remembered my conversation with the floater on my last night at the hospital. I had tried to dismiss her crazy question about what I would do if Jack did not come home. She'd persisted in saying that I needed a backup plan, just in case things didn't work out. And here I was, living through the painful reality she had imagined.

I thought she should know what had happened to me, so I called the hospital to find out her name. When I reached someone in the office that scheduled the floaters, I described the hours we had worked together that Thursday night.

"Sorry, Barbara," said the administrator. "According to our records, there was no floater on duty with you that night."

"What do you mean? I had a conversation with her," I said, and I described what she looked like.

"I'm sorry, Barbara. We don't have any floaters who match that description," she said. "Our records show that you worked alone that night."

Was my floater an angel? Was she sent to caution me on that last night and make me strong? I will never know. But I will never forget that night or our conversation, either.

CHAPTER EIGHT

AT THE END OF my two weeks in Oklahoma, I stopped crying, and I knew I was ready to head back home. I got on the train to St. Louis with 50 cents in my pocket and a shoebox full of fried chicken and an orange. In those days, 50 cents wasn't bad. I thought I could get through the day without needing more.

A very nice man was in the seat next to me. He said he worked for the Baldwin Piano Company in Cincinnati and had been on a sales trip. I told him that I had been to visit my grandmother in Tulsa, and that my mom was meeting me at the train station in Cincinnati. He took me to lunch in the dining car, and we talked all the way to St. Louis.

In St. Louis, we changed trains and continued our conversation. Most of the time, I listened as he told me stories about his family. When we got off the train in Cincinnati, he carried my suitcase for me. I introduced him to my mother, and he told her how nice it had been to talk with me. He said I'd made the trip so much more pleasant. He had certainly made the trip more pleasant for me. It was as if someone had sent him to take care of me, like another guardian angel. And I still had my 50 cents in my pocket.

The two weeks away from Cincinnati had given me time to think about the future. The bottom had fallen out of my life, but I was still standing. So I wouldn't be Mrs. Jack Schier. It wasn't going to be the end of the world for me. Once again, the prospect of becoming a nurse kept me on track and focused on my future. I quickly placed an order for new name tags.

When I got back to the dorm, all my friends acted as if nothing had happened. It was as if there had never been a Jack or a wedding or a cancellation or anything. I can only assume they'd spent a lot of time talking about it while I was away, and their silence was a way of showing their support. My friends were terrific; I don't know how

I could have gotten through it all without them. They'd even taken the time to sew my old name tags, the ones that read "Miss Wells," back on my uniforms. I guess they threw the ones with "Mrs. Barbara Schier" in the trash, and that was fine with me. They had also gone through my room and thrown away all the photographs of Jack. Although that made me a little sad, I knew it was time to move on.

There was only one thing my friends had overlooked: a pair of evening gloves. A nurse in the dorm had loaned me a pair of white silk gloves for the wedding. When I gave them back, she felt so terrible for me, I had to spend the next few minutes trying to cheer her up. She asked if she could help me in any way, and I said no. Everything else had been taken care of. I was almost happy to have the errand of returning the gloves, because it gave me a sense of closure.

Before I left for Oklahoma, my mom had placed an ad in the local newspaper announcing the cancellation of our wedding. In those days, with very little television news, everybody read the newspaper from front page to back. One doctor hadn't seen the ad; he had shown up at the church, and our minister had had to explain what had happened. My mom lost the deposits she'd given the photographer and the bakery for the cake, and I lost all the money I had put into my wedding dress. It had already been altered, and I never picked it up.

Seniors were allowed to move out of the dorm, so for the rest of my final year of nursing school, I lived with a nurse named Nancy. She had an apartment and was looking for someone to split the rent. Nancy seemed like a nice girl, but I didn't know much about her. I didn't know she had boyfriends. Plural. Lots of boyfriends. Boyfriends she slept with. None of my other friends were sleeping with men, so Nancy's behavior was a bit of an eye-opener for me.

And we shared a bedroom, so my sleeping arrangements were dependent on the success or failure of Nancy's love life. If I came home from work and our bedroom door was closed, that meant I was sleeping on the couch. After a while, I stashed a blanket and pillow in the living room closet so I would be prepared for the inevitable.

We all knew that after graduation, we could have a job at The Jewish Hospital if we wanted it. We could almost pick which floor we wanted to work on. I had already decided that I wanted to work on my friend Norma Kaye's floor. By then, she had graduated and was head nurse on the floor for cardiac cases. These were among the most critical patients in the hospital, requiring 24-hour care.

Now that my relationship with Jack was over, I had to contemplate dating again. I had never really dated anyone other than Jack. Jesse Ellington, who I dated in eighth and ninth grade, was just a nice guy I met through my friend Anita, who lived in the apartment building where Jesse lived with his grandmother. But Jesse was just a friend, not a serious boyfriend like Jack. I had danced with some of the morticians at our nursing school dances, but that was about it. From time to time, a doctor at the hospital would ask me out, but I always made it clear that I had a boyfriend. If a doctor asked me out now, when I didn't have a boyfriend, would I say yes or no?

While I was engaged to Jack, there was this older doctor, I'll call him Dr. O, who worked on the same floor I did. He would say things like "Ready for coffee, Miss Wells?" or "Where should we have dinner tonight?" He was a married man with children, and when he asked me out, which he often did, I would remind him that I was engaged. When I came back from Oklahoma, that was no longer true.

Dr. O came to my parents' house and sat at the kitchen table with me. He didn't stay long, but he wanted me to know how sorry he was and to be supportive. I thanked him, saying I just had to get on with the rest of my life. Returning to my job at the hospital seemed a good way to start. I needed a schedule and a structure to my day so I would not waste any more time being sad.

One night around 11, as I was coming off duty, I bumped into Norma Kaye and her friend Phyllis. A group of doctors were waiting in a car at the front of the hospital to take them out. I surprised myself by saying, "Can I come?"

As I climbed into the car, I saw that one of the doctors was Dr. O. Looking back, I find it interesting that he was ready to go out on the town with Norma and Phyllis when he had made it clear he had designs on me. At the time, I didn't give it a second thought.

We had a great time that night, and after that he started pursuing me seriously. I felt he was a very kind, sweet man. Eventually, he wanted to take me someplace to have sex. His aunt, who was a patient in the hospital, had a lovely apartment nearby. I had never slept with a man, and I was happy I had made the decision for him to be my first.

Over the next few months, we spent a lot of time together and started going on regular dates. He told me about his three children and his wife, whom he had divorced and then married again. Even though Dr. O was married, and 25 years older than I, he was so nice to me, at a time in my life when I needed to be with a kind man. After his aunt left the hospital, we usually met at the apartments of some of his doctor friends.

When we were together and he was on call, he would tell the switchboard operator that he was resting in the hospital, but he wouldn't say where. Then he would dash off down the street to be with me. If the switchboard operator beeped him, he would rush back to the hospital to respond to his pager. It was exciting to be with him, because I could never be sure when he would come or go.

There was a point when I thought I could be happy for the rest of my life just to be the mistress of Dr. O. I didn't really think about kids, and after crashing and burning with Jack, I wasn't that keen on marriage, either.

Things began to shift when I became better friends with Donna, who had graduated from nursing school the previous year. She was still doing kidney research, and once I graduated, I worked on that floor next to her patients. She had just ended a bad relationship and was ready for a major change. She had dreams of working in another country, and one afternoon she suggested that we become nurses in Mexico.

Dr. O didn't like the idea, but the more I thought about it, the more sense it made. If I went to Mexico with Donna, I would have an opportunity for a new future. If I stayed in Cincinnati, I would just remain Dr. O's mistress.

He wanted to be with me, but he was honest about what he could offer. "I want you to be happy," he said. "But I will never be able to pick out kitchen curtains with you."

That statement made me pause, because ultimately, I did want a husband to pick out curtains with. And after Donna and I made the decision to go to Mexico, Dr. O got a little strange. He would sit outside my apartment to see if I came in or went out with other men. He acted as if I were his possession. I decided to cool things off and start seeing other men. One night, I came back to my apartment with a date, and Dr. O was waiting in his car. When my date left, Dr. O knocked on my door and told me how angry he was. Moving to Mexico was looking better and better. As was seeing other men.

One night when I was working the 11 p.m. to 7 a.m. shift, a doctor came in to say goodbye to everyone on my floor. Dr. Paul Stein—we all called him Pinky—was going to Panama to do a residency in heart surgery. He had to drive his car to New York to meet his ship. We were just friends, but when he came to say goodbye to me, he said, "What are you doing tomorrow?" I told him I was working. He said, "Why don't you get someone to cover your shift and drive to New York City with me?" I could help with the driving, he said, and then he would give me a plane ticket home.

His offer made me realize all the places I had never been in my life, so impulsively I said yes. He was single and so was I, and I thought it would be a fun weekend. I called the head nurse on the floor I worked on, as well as the director of the school, and told them that Dr. Pinky Stein needed someone to drive with him to New York, and I had volunteered for the job. I made it sound very official, like it was important hospital business.

At 2 a.m., I called my mother and told her I was going to New York City for a few days and asked her to pick me up at the airport when I returned. Then I ran back to the dorm and woke up a few girls, who helped me pack. We all wore similar sizes, so I packed my suitcase with everyone's best dresses and headed off to meet Pinky.

Pinky had said that his mother and aunt were going to be with us, but it soon became clear that it was just the two of us. I was driving to New York to spend the weekend in a hotel with a doctor. I was very well liked, and I think my friends just wanted me to be happy. They knew what had happened with Jack and thought I deserved better.

We drove to New York City and checked into the Warwick Hotel. The minute we entered the hotel room, he was all over me. We ordered champagne, shared a bubble bath, and carried on for two days. I had never stayed in a big hotel or ordered room service. We toured the city, walking to Times Square and Chinatown. The trip was so romantic that sleeping with a man I hardly knew seemed part of the magic. The experience turned out to be everything I had imagined having an affair in New York would be. We knew that we might never see each other again, and that made the weekend even more exciting.

My first visit to New York City was in 1960. I went on a road trip with Dr. Paul "Pinky" Stein, and we stayed at a fancy hotel in Manhattan. At the end of the trip, he boarded a cruise ship to Panama, where he had a residency in heart surgery.

That was my first of many wonderful trips to New York City. After I left Pinky at the pier, I walked all the way back to the hotel, thrilled by the energy of this exciting city.

When Pinky reported to the ship, I went to a party onboard with him. The captain was very flirty. "Why don't you come with us?" he said. Even after that weekend, the idea of sailing off to Panama for two years sounded crazy. "I need to go back and graduate from nursing school," I said.

So I said my goodbyes to Pinky and headed back to the hotel. Unfortunately, the city's taxi drivers were on strike, so I had to walk all the way from the dock, alone, in my high heels. My feet were killing me, but I didn't let that ruin my good mood. I imagined I was an actress in a wonderful romantic movie, walking back to my fancy hotel to check out, and that weekends in New York City were a regular treat for me. The trip gave me a taste of what it would be like to be on my own in Mexico. There were so many places to see in the world. That weekend in New York was just the beginning.

Back in Cincinnati, Dr. O had found out about my trip and was furious, which made me grow even more tired of him. I also was getting tired of Nancy and her dates and sleeping on the couch every night. Even though it wouldn't be long before I graduated, I decided to move into a furnished apartment with Donna. She had been working as a nanny for a doctor named Osher and his wife, who had five boys. They had helped Donna apply to nursing school. They owned a small apartment above Dr. Osher's medical offices and let us live there for free—we didn't even have to pay the gas, electric, or telephone bills, because they were going to tear down the building after the first of the year. We planned to leave for Mexico in January, so it was a case of perfect timing.

After talking with some Mexican doctors at The Jewish Hospital, we set our sights on Mexico City. Neither of us spoke Spanish, but the doctors had told us that many people who worked in the hospitals were bilingual, and we could certainly get jobs. Unfortunately, when I called the Mexican consulate to ask about visas, the woman I spoke with said that Mexico City was inundated with American nurses, and they weren't hiring any more.

The thought of staying in Cincinnati for the rest of our lives depressed us both, and we still wanted to go someplace sunny and warm. Donna had a friend from high school named Jerry who was living in Los Angeles and worked as a reservationist for one of the airlines. When we called him, he promised to let us stay with him until we found an apartment. Then we asked some doctors at The Jewish Hospital to recommend a hospital in L.A., and many suggested Cedars of Lebanon. Some of them had done their residencies there. When Donna and I wrote to Cedars, we were hired right away. Now all we had to do was save money for the trip west.

We each earned $300 a month. We squirreled away money from our paychecks, and by the end of December, we had enough to buy two one-way plane tickets to California, with about $300 each left over.

Dr. O wasn't the only one who was upset I was leaving. My mother was angry, too. No member of my family had ever lived on the West Coast, and she thought I was insane to even think of such a thing. She worried if I lived in California, I would be shot and killed. She even bought a brand-new Chevrolet in an effort to entice me to stay. Our family had never owned a car before. Not even a Chevy, however, was going to stop me.

Many of our friends also wondered why Donna and I would want to move away. Most were perfectly content to stay in Ohio forever, to work as nurses until they married and then quit to raise their children. They could not understand why we would give up safe jobs at The Jewish Hospital to work in a city where we knew no one but some guy named Jerry.

Donna and I left for California on January 16, 1961, a very snowy day. Even so, we had our hair done that morning and dressed in black cocktail dresses and white gloves for the plane. In those days, people dressed up when they flew, and we wanted to fit in. My mother was taking us to the airport at 10 a.m. To my surprise, Dr. O showed up about 8 a.m. and begged me to stay. There I was, packed and dressed to go to California, and he was offering me anything I wanted. I was firm with him. I told him that I was going, and that he

A composite of my graduating class from nursing school. I am on the far right, third from the bottom.

My graduation portrait. I still have my cap and even wore it in one of Garry's movies.

In 1960, I graduated from The Jewish Hospital of Cincinnati School of Nursing.

should leave before my mother arrived.

My whole family took Donna and me to the airport to say goodbye: my mom, my dad, my two sisters, two brothers, a cousin, and a dog. We got on the plane and settled into our seats, so excited to finally be on our way. Suddenly, we heard screaming from the back of the plane, where people were still boarding. It was my mother, screaming and yelling, "Barbara Sue! Don't go! Please don't go!" I stood up and pushed through the people moving forward to give her another hug and usher her off the plane. Donna and I were holding our breath as it lifted into the sky.

Cincinnati was the only city I had ever called home, but as I watched the buildings below grow smaller and smaller, I knew I would never call it home again. It was time to carve out a new life. It would be a life without Jack. It would be a life without Dr. O. It would be a life away from my family. It would be a life in California. I couldn't wait for the plane to land so I could get started.

CHAPTER NINE

WHEN WE LANDED, IT was 11 o'clock at night, but the lights were bright and Los Angeles seemed the most exciting place in the world. Jerry picked us up in his convertible. We climbed up on the back seats and rode down Sunset Boulevard in style, as if we were in a parade, as he drove past places like Dino's, Dean Martin's restaurant, which we had only seen on television.

Jerry drove us to a Japanese restaurant called Yamashiro, which overlooked all of Hollywood. We had drinks and toasted our arrival. When it dawned on me that I hadn't called my mother yet, I quickly found a payphone and told her everything was fine on my first night in California.

Jerry and his roommate let us sleep in their king-size bed while they slept on the living room couches. Despite the fact that they shared a bedroom, it didn't occur to Donna or me that Jerry was gay. We didn't know until about a year later. Until then, we didn't even know what being gay was.

Jerry was a better host than we ever could have imagined. He fed us and took us apartment hunting after he got off work. He was so nice. He really made sure we knew our way around town.

After two weeks, Donna and I found an apartment in a complex called Barnsdall Terrace, on Edgemont Avenue. It was in a beautiful new building with a gorgeous swimming pool, and the rent was $150 a month. To sign the lease, we needed to pay the first and last months' rent. After Donna and I each paid $150, we were left with a grand total of $16. To celebrate the new apartment, we splurged on a set of purple sheets, which pretty much left us without a dime. We didn't think this was a problem, because we were about to start our jobs at Cedars of Lebanon.

We soon learned that new nurses at Cedars didn't get their first paychecks for three weeks. During those weeks, we could barely make ends meet, but we were too embarrassed to tell anyone. We often got through the day by eating cups of Jell-O and pudding out of a refrigerator at the hospital. It was for the patients, but nobody seemed to mind if we ate from it occasionally. We had to be creative, and that food was free and easy to get.

We were strapped for other things, though, like toothpaste, shampoo, soap, even tampons. There was a big drugstore at the end of our street, and one day we went in wearing our uniforms and caps. The place was empty except for a pharmacist, an older man with a gentle smile. When we told him that we'd just started working at Cedars and wouldn't get paid for three weeks, he thought the timing was interesting, because his wife was currently a patient on the sixth floor. His grin grew wider when I told him that I worked on the sixth floor.

The pharmacist's name was Harry Skepner, and his wife, Kay, was recovering from gall bladder surgery that very morning. He asked if I could check on her and make sure she had everything she needed. I said, "Of course," and that's when he told us to buy whatever we needed in his drugstore, and not to worry about paying anything until our first paychecks arrived. We couldn't believe our good luck. Before we left, we ran through the store on a shopping spree.

I found Kay right where her husband had said she would be, recovering from gall bladder surgery on the sixth floor. We hit it off right from the start. In fact, we got along so well that when she was discharged, she asked me to be her private-duty nurse for two weeks while she was on bed rest. The recuperation period for removing a gall bladder then was much longer. The incisions were very big.

Every day around 3 p.m., when my shift was over, Harry would pick me up and drive me to his home. I usually ate dinner with the family, too. They had two children: a daughter in college and a son who was trying to break into the business side of Hollywood. Sometimes I would sleep over, and Harry would drive me to work the next day.

Over the next few months, Kay became the mother I had always imagined having. She taught me all the ins and outs of cooking and entertaining. She taught me how to set the table for a formal dinner party. She taught me how to make a brisket from scratch. She taught me how to make matzo ball soup, a dish I had never even tasted before. Being with Kay was like taking a crash course in how to become a lady. She was so refined in everything she did, and very patient with my lack of knowledge about everyday things. I fell so in love with the family that I even went on a few dates with Kay and Harry's son, just because it made me feel part of the family.

Once my first paycheck arrived, my new life was full speed ahead. Donna and I didn't have a car, but we lived close enough to walk to the hospital. Most nurses didn't have medical insurance, but doctors in the hospital saw us for free, as a courtesy. I don't remember paying for any appointments. Aside from our rent, all we had to pay was the phone and gas-and-electric bills. Donna set aside money each month to send to her family back in Indiana. We didn't have checking accounts but kept our money in the sock drawer of our dresser. We didn't have credit cards, either, so we paid for everything in cash from the sock drawer. (Years later, when I was married, I got my first credit card, for 76 gasoline.) If we were out shopping and found a dress we liked, we would buy it on layaway and pay $10 or $20 toward the total cost each month.

My biggest expense was the telephone bill. Dr. O would call me collect, so his wife couldn't trace the call, and we would talk for hours. During my first month in Los Angeles, I felt a little homesick and nostalgic for my life in Ohio, and I looked forward to his phone calls. But I began to feel he was intruding on my new life. Talking to him was preventing me from going out and meeting new people. Sometimes he would call just to see if I had a date over. He acted as if he could control me, even though we were 2,000 miles and half a dozen states apart.

I finally wised up to the fact that I couldn't spend piles of money on long-distance phone calls for a relationship with a very married man. I told Dr. O that I didn't want him to call me anymore. If I was ever going to break things off with him, it had to be done right. When he persisted, I said that I wouldn't see him again until I was married and pregnant with my first child.

Donna and I usually worked different shifts. I might work from 7 a.m. to 3 p.m., and she would work from 3 p.m. to 11 p.m., or 11 p.m. to 7 a.m. That suited both of us, because our apartment was really small and it was nice to be home alone. If a nurse didn't come in or the hospital needed extra staffing, we often worked double shifts.

Unlike at The Jewish Hospital, we didn't socialize with the doctors much. But for our first Thanksgiving in California, a wealthy doctor and his wife invited all the nurses who didn't have plans for the holiday to come to their home. That Thanksgiving was one I will never forget. We had driven by Beverly Hills mansions, but I had never been inside one. When we stepped into the doctor's beautiful house, there was a big Thanksgiving buffet table awaiting us, with silver candlesticks, crystal glasses, and cloth napkins—everything I thought a formal dinner party should have, just like the dinner parties Kay had described.

At one point, the doctor's wife clinked a spoon on her glass and raised it. She said, "I would like to welcome all you lovely nurses into our home. It's a pleasure to meet all of you, and we're so happy you could share Thanksgiving with us."

The doctor and his wife didn't have any children, and I think this was their way of giving back, to people who couldn't be with their families. I thought it was the best Thanksgiving dinner ever.

That first year at Cedars, Donna and I made a group of close friends, who were scattered around the hospital on different floors. One of the things that drew us together was our age—we were much younger than most of the other head nurses or floor nurses, many of whom looked like they were pushing past 70. Our friends included Peggy and Sara, who had come from Indiana together; Joan, who was from Cleveland; and Cyl, from Pittsburgh. There was also Barbara, a younger nurse doing her rotation at the hospital. She had grown up in Glendale, which was close by. Her parents still lived there, and they helped us navigate Los Angeles. They helped me get my first dentist, for example. Another thing that bonded our group was that the hospital put us in charge of opening the first intensive-care unit in Los Angeles. These new critical-care units were being created in big cities across the country, so we knew we were participating in something groundbreaking and exciting. It helped that many of us were friends already, so we were able to work as a team from the start.

We had three months to learn what we needed to know to open the unit. We had to catch up on a lot, because in those days, nurses didn't start IVs (intravenous devices) or read EKGs (electrocardiograms) or provide many other now-routine treatments. In addition to having to learn all that, we helped design the layout: where the beds would be placed, where the equipment would be set up, etc.

We started with eight beds in a circle, with the nurses' desk at the top of the circle. All the linens, medicine, and equipment were behind the desk. Today, doctors and nurses use an array of high-tech equipment to monitor a patient's vital signs. Back then, all we had was an oscilloscope, or silo scope. As much as we relied on it, it didn't provide much information. It simply told us if the patient's heart was beating or not.

When construction was complete, we prepared to open the unit at 7 a.m. Necessity changed that plan. In the middle of the night, Dr. Josh Fields, a heart surgeon at the hospital, telephoned and said, "How would you like to open the unit tonight?" At first, Donna and I balked at the idea, because all the plans were set. The hospital had arranged for newspaper reporters to cover the opening, and we were looking forward to that. But Dr. Fields said he had a patient who needed us now, so we threw on our clothes and headed to the hospital.

And at 3 a.m., without much fanfare or celebration, Donna and I opened the first intensive-care unit at Cedars of Lebanon Hospital. Although it started quietly, before most people were awake, it would be in the spotlight from then on. Not only did reporters arrive later that day, they wrote about the unit over the next several years as

With my longtime best friends Peggy, Donna, Elaine, and Joan in 1988.

celebrities, politicians, and other dignitaries came and went through its doors. Our very special unit served as a model for other critical-care units that opened in hospitals around the country.

When we weren't restarting hearts at Cedars, Donna and I had fun just being single in Los Angeles. We went swimming. We played tennis. We loved having people over for dinner parties. We liked making fancy hors d'oeuvres, like escargot and pickled herring. We didn't really know how to cook, but we would see pictures in magazines and try to duplicate the recipes for our friends or whoever we were dating at the time.

Two of our best friends were a couple in our building. In our complex, there were two penthouses, and Pamela and Luigi lived in one of them. They were in the restaurant business and worked nights, so we often saw them by the pool before our evening shifts. Luigi was a maître d' and Pamela was a waitress, they said, working at a local Italian restaurant where stars like Frank Sinatra and Dean Martin liked to dine. As far as we were concerned, they were the closest we had gotten to movie stars, so we considered them almost stars themselves.

When they weren't in their apartment or by the pool, they were working. They didn't seem to have other friends and often invited us for dinner at their apartment. Although we spent plenty of time with them, they remained mysterious. Their story came out in little glimpses. For example, we had assumed they were married, but it turned out they were not. We assumed neither had any family and eventually learned that Pamela was divorced and had three children. They lived with her mother, but we never saw them visit.

One of the most intriguing things about Pamela and Luigi is that they seemed to have endless amounts of money. Donna and I were so naive, we figured they made it all in the restaurant business. Pamela was a very good seamstress, and she would sometimes buy very expensive fabric and make fancy gowns for herself. Then one day, Luigi came home and announced he was designing a new restaurant for Jerry Lewis. After that, Pamela started buying expensive wigs and jewelry. Donna and I couldn't wait to see what she was going to wear next. The two of them looked so glamorous together and seemed to be so much in love.

Not long after Luigi opened Jerry Lewis's restaurant, Pamela stopped working and Luigi bought her a white Cadillac. But shortly after the white Cadillac arrived, Luigi disappeared. We didn't ask many questions, and Pamela didn't offer any explanation. She simply said that she came home one day and all of his clothes were gone.

The next week, two shady-looking characters came around to the apartment complex and demanded money from her. She didn't have any money, so they took her white Cadillac and everything else she owned, including her furniture, her jewelry, even her wigs.

With nothing left, Pamela had no choice but to go live with her mother and children. Luigi disappeared for the next 15 years. We never found out what he was really doing. We assumed it had something to do with the Mafia, but we'll never know. Donna and I were two small-town girls from the Midwest, and for us, watching the demise of Pamela and Luigi's life was like seeing a Hollywood movie unfold. The last we heard, Pamela was working at a hot dog stand.

CHAPTER TEN

WHEN DONNA AND I hadn't been hanging out with Pamela and Luigi, we went on dates with doctors. It wasn't that we specifically wanted to date doctors, but doctors were the only single men we met. A problem was that many of the doctors who wanted to date us weren't single. After my long relationship with Dr. O, I didn't want anything to do with a married man. I'd rather stay home and watch a movie on television than go out with a married man.

Even when I went on dates, it was never very serious. For a little while, I dated a veterinarian who was best friends with Mort, a doctor Donna was dating at the time. They were from Columbus, Ohio. Donna and I were so poor, often we went on dates just so we could have a nice dinner and go to a movie. I remember when a new Elvis Presley movie came out. We waited until one of the single doctors asked us out, and when he asked what we wanted to do, we said, "Let's go see *Blue Hawaii*."

I didn't have much time for a serious relationship anyway. My hours were so long that most of the time I simply ate and slept at the apartment, then headed back to work. I figured when Mr. Right was out there, he would come and find me. Until then, I was going to concentrate on being the best nurse I could. That, and saving enough money so I could stop eating Jell-O and pudding out of the patients' refrigerator.

In the 1960s, the rules about nursing were very strict. You couldn't wear your hair on your neck. If you had long hair, you wore it securely pinned or tied up and back. We heard that if the head nurse saw your hair down, she would cut it off. I never actually saw this happen, but it was a rumor none of the nurses wanted to put to the test.

You couldn't wear any jewelry except a wedding ring and a regulation nurses' watch, with a second hand that was used to take a patient's pulse. Watches decorated with jewels or had fancy parts to them were strictly forbidden. Lipstick and powder were allowed, but no fingernail polish and no long fingernails. Your nail was not supposed to be visible beyond the tip of your finger.

The list went on and on. No colored sweaters. No dirty sweaters. No dirty shoes. The uniform was clear: sparkling white shoes, white stockings, white dress, and white sweater. No colored surgical scrubs worn outside the operating room, and under no circumstances in the cafeteria. When I see nurses today, I see them wearing colorful sweaters full of germs. I see them wearing scrubs to the supermarket and to pick up their kids and then back into the hospital. I think the days of the all-white uniforms were much safer and cleaner for both nurses and patients.

While there were many rules for nurses, at Cedars all bets were off when it came to celebrities. Celebrities loved having their medical procedures and treatments done at Cedars, and Cedars loved having them there. Most floors had wards of ten beds or more, but the celebrity floor had only private rooms. Private-duty nurses staffed these rooms and often helped with recovery and rehabilitation when the patients were released. Those nurses were in some of the most glamorous mansions in Beverly Hills, Bel Air, and Brentwood.

When movie stars checked into Cedars, they were given the royal treatment. One day when I went to get some fresh sheets, I found a man wearing a tuxedo and holding a violin. "What are you doing in my linen closet?" I said.

"Tuning my violin," he said.

"But why?" I asked.

"I'm going to play for Elizabeth and Richard's dinner."

"Elizabeth and Richard?" I said.

"Liz Taylor and Richard Burton," he explained. "They want some romantic music while they dine by candlelight."

Catered food, full bars, and, yes, even violins were permitted when a celebrity was in Cedars. I didn't work on the celebrity floor, so my run-ins with movie stars were few and far between, but often more memorable.

One day, a hospital pharmacist I had befriended called to tell me that Frank Sinatra was due to be admitted any minute. The pharmacy, which was on the bottom floor, had a secret door at the back that special people used to avoid reporters and photographers at the hospital's front entrance. I asked another nurse to cover for me and ran downstairs just in time to see Sinatra coming through the secret door. I had never seen him in person and was shocked to see what a short little man he was. I had assumed he would be a towering figure, but I was certainly wrong. He was no taller than the pharmacist himself, which was not saying much.

The biggest celebrity during my tenure at Cedars was one I would never meet. In August 1962, we got the call that Marilyn Monroe was being rushed to the hospital after a drug overdose. We prepared the gurney for her and waited anxiously in the intensive-care unit. Sadly, she died on the way to the hospital. While throngs of reporters waited outside the front doors, the ambulance took Marilyn directly to the coroner's office. We never got the chance to try to save her life. I thought if she had been found sooner and had gotten to the hospital earlier, we might have had a chance to bring her back. But we'll never know, because time wasn't on her side.

On more than one occasion, however, we brought the great comic actor Peter Sellers back to life. He came into the intensive-care unit after his first heart attack. He was plagued by a condition that caused his heart to stop beating. Because we used an oscilloscope, we knew when a heart had stopped. When this happened with Sellers, one of us would jump on his bed, straddle him, and pound on his chest until his heart started again. I personally restarted his heart about ten times, and I was just one of many nurses who worked on him over the years. Every time he left the unit, he would give each nurse an autographed picture and thank us for taking care of him. More than any other celebrity, Sellers was considered a "regular," like a customer in a coffee shop who shows up again and again for a refill.

Another celebrity regular was an actress named Marilyn Maxwell, who appeared in many films and radio programs and had entertained troops on USO tours with Bob Hope. She had kidney problems, and when she was at Cedars, she always wanted a room away from the celebrity floor and right by a nurses' station. She was fond of giving presents to the nurses. Once, she gave me a beautiful pair of earrings.

Her best friend was Rock Hudson. He came to visit her nearly every day and would always bring a box of chocolates for the nurses. Most celebrities treated the nurses like servants, but he was different. He knew all our names, which impressed me. He would say, "Miss Wells! How nice to see you!" And then he would give me a big hug, as if we were old friends. All the nurses at Cedars thought Rock Hudson was the most charming actor we had ever met.

One night, a patient was brought in at 10:45. I never liked getting a new patient as I headed off duty, but he was clearly having a heart attack. My floor was mostly for surgical patients, but we had an open bed and the cardiac floor didn't. I took the man's blood pressure and tried to keep him calm. This proved to be challenging, because his wife was throwing herself around the room and having a fit.

I really couldn't think much about her comfort, because I was trying to tend to her husband. But she kept saying, "Where's my room? I want a private room! Where's my room?" Finally, after reaching the end of my rope, I turned around to her and said, "I am trying to take care of your husband. Please get out of here. I will take care of you later." I escorted her out of the room and closed the door, then turned my attention back to her husband.

About ten minutes later, the supervisor of the hospital came into the room and said, "Miss Wells, can you please come out in the hall?" I worried that my patient would die if I left, but the supervisor had someone cover for me and insisted I step outside. The supervisor told me that I had just thrown Jennifer Jones out of the room.

"Who?" I said.

"You don't know?" said the supervisor, surprised. "She is a very famous actress."

I thought if she was such a famous actress, she should act a little better in a hospital, but I didn't say anything. I apologized and said it wouldn't happen again. Her husband at the time was David O. Selznick, a well-known film producer and studio executive. He died a few years later of a blocked coronary artery.

I was not used to getting yelled at, especially when I hadn't done anything wrong, at least in my opinion. In fact, the only time I ever made a medical mistake was during my senior year at The Jewish Hospital. I was on the night shift and it was about 6:30 a.m., so my shift was just about over. One of my responsibilities before going home was to give insulin shots to all the patients who needed them. We had practiced giving shots to oranges for many weeks, and we all felt at ease with the procedure.

I said something like "Here's your shot" to my final patient and immediately realized I had injected the wrong patient. This patient did not require insulin. I hurried to the nursing station and called the doctor on duty, and he went with me to talk to her. I told her how sorry I was and quickly explained that she was not in any medical danger. She was probably going to get hungry—very hungry—but there would be no other side effects.

I filled out an incident report and waited for my nursing supervisor to come on duty so that I could tell her. Ultimately, it was probably good that I'd made that error, because I never made a mistake like that again.

CHAPTER ELEVEN

I KNEW IN MY heart that I wanted to plan a wedding again someday. However, I wasn't exactly in an arena full of eligible men at Cedars. I worked with male doctors, but most were already married. And in those days, it was frowned upon to make friends with your patients. We weren't even supposed to tell them our first names. My name tag read "Miss Wells," and that is what my patients called me. So that was not an option, either.

I had promised myself I would not go out with another married man. Unfortunately, I did from time to time, because some of my dates lied. Mike was doing his residency in gastroenterology when he asked me on a date to Griffith Observatory. Just before he was supposed to pick me up, a friend told me about him.

When I got into his car, I said, "I heard a little something about you today."

"What is that?" he asked innocently.

"I heard that you might be married," I said. "Is that true?"

"Yes, I am," he said. I was surprised he came clean so quickly.

"I'm sorry, but you have to turn the car around."

"Really?"

"Right now."

"Why?" he asked, genuinely confused.

"I was involved once with a married man, and it is a waste of my time. You are charming and wonderful, but you are married. I hope we can be friends, but right now I want to go home."

He took me home, and the next week he started dating Donna. She didn't date him for very long, either. We agreed that he was very charming, yet very unavailable.

That's when I decided I wanted to join the Peace Corps. I had never known anyone who had worked in the Peace Corps, but I thought it sounded interesting and worthwhile. It was 1962, and for someone who wanted to contribute to society and had no "significant other," it looked like a promising possibility.

I imagined being sent someplace I'd never been, which could have been pretty much anywhere. Before moving to California, I had left Ohio only for brief trips to Kentucky, Oklahoma, Atlantic City, and New York. When people talked about England or France, they could have been talking about the moon as far as I was concerned. I was the least-traveled person I knew, and the Peace Corps looked like a golden opportunity to combine service and travel.

That summer, Donna was dating a man who lived with a roommate in Barnsdall Gardens, the apartments next door to Barnsdall Terrace. Tommy and Donna were forever trying to set me up with their friends so they could have our apartment to themselves.

Tommy, who had graduated from Northwestern, near Chicago, had introduced me to several of his friends, but I didn't find any of them interesting. He was relentless in his questions about my love life.

"So who are you dating now?" he asked one night.

"I'm dating a doctor. Leave me alone," I said. "I've dated enough of your friends."

"What about at the party?" Tommy persisted. "Did you meet Garry?"

Tommy had thrown a party earlier that month for two friends who moved to Los Angeles and had just flown in from New York.

"I only met Fred," I said.

"What? You didn't meet Garry? That was the guy I wanted you to meet."

"The guy sleeping on the bed with the coats? He never woke up," I said. "Maybe he was jetlagged?"

"Well, then, you have to meet him right now," said Tommy.

He ran back to his apartment, grabbed Garry, and brought him to ours. I was pissed. Donna was home, so I walked into the kitchen and started grilling a steak. I heard the three of them in the living room talking about taking a trip to Las Vegas. I had never been to

Las Vegas but had often heard about it from Pamela and Luigi. I thought, "What am I doing? I should be social. And Garry is kind of cute." So I went into the living room and introduced myself to Garry Marshall.

Garry was a struggling comedy writer who had moved to L.A. to write for the first season of *The Joey Bishop Show*. The four of us went out for drinks at Yamashiro, the restaurant where Donna and I had gone on our first night in L.A. While Donna and Tommy were reading their menus, Garry leaned over and gave me a quick kiss on the cheek. I knew then that he liked me, and that we would definitely see each other again.

When he asked me out a few days later, we went to a restaurant called The Cameo, where we sat at the bar and had drinks. This was new to me, because "good girls" didn't sit at bars, and I found it glamorous. Garry was very funny and tried out some jokes on me.

To impress him, I began a long and involved joke, but I kept losing my way. Garry helped me by saying the punchline, which surprised me.

"Oh! You saw the same show I did?" I asked.

"No," he said. "I wrote that joke."

He had written it when he worked on Jack Paar's *Tonight Show*, when he was living in New York. After that, I tried to leave the joke telling to Garry.

To be honest, I was not free as a bird when I met him. I was dating Josh Fields, the heart surgeon I met when we opened the critical-care unit. We were not exactly an exclusive item. We would go to dinner and sleep together afterward, or he would call me at 3 a.m. and I would put on a trench coat and go to his apartment. I liked the spontaneity, though it felt very on-again-off-again with Josh.

One Friday afternoon, the phone rang. "Barbara, I'm glad you're home. Let's take a road trip to Bakersfield," Josh said. "I'm giving a speech at a conference, and we will have a hotel room for the weekend. You can drive while I write the speech in the car."

It didn't matter that Bakersfield was not the sexiest city to visit, or that I would do all the driving. It was exciting to think I would be taking a road trip with a man in his Thunderbird and staying in a hotel. And Garry and I had not made any plans for the weekend yet.

I threw my clothes in a bag and hopped behind the wheel of Josh's car. When we got to the hotel, he went right into the conference and told me to drive around for a few hours, and then he would check us in. I had never been to Bakersfield and had no GPS, of course, or even a map. I just kept making big circles around the hotel so I could remember where it was and not get lost.

A few hours later, Josh was at the front of the hotel, and we got our room and ordered room service. We lounged by the pool the next day, had another nice dinner that night, and headed home on Sunday. I'd had no other place to be, and it seemed a civilized way to spend a weekend away from Los Angeles.

When I walked into my apartment that night, the phone was ringing. "Where have you been?"

"Garry?"

"I have been calling you all weekend. Where have you been?" he repeated.

"I've been out and about," I said, not wanting to go into any details.

"I was worried," he said. It dawned on me that he was getting serious, and I should pay a little more attention to him.

About a week later, my friend Barbara Hauptman and I were walking down the street and I saw Garry coming toward us.

"There he is," I said.

"Who?" said Barbara.

"The guy I'm sort of seeing," I said.

"The guy...with the *ice cream*?"

Garry was eating a fudgesicle, in a plaid blazer and black boots. I thought he looked so cute walking down the street like that. It was at that moment that I thought maybe I should start seeing him exclusively. I had a feeling that it was more important to date a kind and consistent man and I should stop seeing doctors.

Garry and I were as different as night and day. I was from the

Midwest; he was from an East Coast neighborhood known as the Bronx, specifically, the Grand Concourse. I was from a very large family with legions of Baptist ancestors in Kentucky. Garry was from a small family with Italian roots and relatives still living in Abruzzi. I was an excellent driver, well versed at road trips. He was a terrible driver, who had finally gotten his driver's license after three tries. I ate just about anything and was certainly not picky. Garry was allergic to almost 200 different foods and pollens. He said that when he was small, his mother used to pray he would marry a doctor. Dating a nurse sounded like a good fit.

If opposites attracted each other, we were a prime example. Garry thought we were well suited from the get-go. If I was feeling blue, he could make me laugh. If he ever got sick, I could save his life. He liked knowing that I had saved Peter Sellers many times. He felt that made me a "friend of comedy." And I could get along with all his friends, too.

There I was, a professional nurse faced with the ultimate challenge: a boyfriend with severe allergies who was also a hypochondriac. During those early months of dating Garry, I wondered if I had met my future husband. I wasn't sure. I was 22 years old and had been in California for only a year. I wasn't sure of many things, especially love. Going into the Peace Corps, however, was definitely off the table.

CHAPTER TWELVE

WITH GARRY, EVERYTHING HAPPENED so quickly. Once I knew he most certainly did not have a wife hiding someplace, things moved at lightning speed. We went from meeting to dating and then from dating to dating exclusively before we really had time to talk about it. And then, before we knew it, we were planning a wedding, or at least talking about getting married.

The funny thing is, I don't remember him ever saying the words "Will you marry me?" One of our first trips alone together was a weekend in Palm Springs. By then, Donna, my best friend, had broken up with Tommy, Garry's best friend. Donna had started dating a hospital administrator, and they were in Palm Springs the same weekend, although they checked into the very chic Riviera Hotel, while Garry and I were at a little off-the-beaten-path place called the Lone Palm. We splurged and paid a few extra dollars to get a television in our room.

On one of our first nights there, we went to a place called the Chi-Chi. It was a Las Vegas-style supper club (once described as "the second biggest nightclub west of the Mississippi"), so we dressed up and treated ourselves to a fancy dinner. While we were eating, Garry turned to me and said, "If you were going to get married, what kind of wedding would you want?"

The truth was that the wedding I had always dreamed of was the wedding I had planned. That was a wedding that would never happen, and over time, it had become a dream I no longer dwelled on.

"Well, I've really never thought about a wedding," I lied. "What kind of wedding would you like?"

He thought for a minute and said, "Something simple. Maybe we would grab a bunch of friends and go to Las Vegas for the weekend?"

"That sounds like fun," I said, trying to be breezy.

The thought hung in the air between us for at least a minute.

Then we moved on to another subject.

When we got back to the hotel, I waited for Garry to go to the bathroom so I could have some privacy. Then I picked up the phone and called Donna at the Riviera. "I think Garry just asked me to marry him," I said.

"Oh, my God. That's not possible!" she said.

She was flabbergasted, because we had been dating less than three months. Most of that time, I was at the hospital and Garry was at the studio writing for *The Joey Bishop Show*. Our schedules were not well aligned. Sometimes, if I had a night off and Garry did not, I would go over to his apartment at Barnsdall Gardens and hang out with his roommate, Richie, who wrote for technical magazines.

When Garry and I returned from Palm Springs, I didn't bring up the marriage subject again, and neither did he. We were more focused on work. Garry worked at Desilu Cahuenga, the lot where Danny Thomas and his producing partner, Sheldon Leonard, shot many of their television shows. (His own popular sit-com, *The Danny Thomas Show*, was the launching pad for *The Joey Bishop Show*, and Thomas was an executive producer.) Desilu was an independent production company that had been founded by Desi Arnaz and Lucille Ball. In the early 1960s, she was filming *The Lucy Show* on another lot, Desilu Gower.

Every Friday, *The Joey Bishop Show* filmed the following week's episode in front of a studio audience on a soundstage at Desilu Cahuenga. Garry wanted me to see what he did for a living, so one Friday I went to watch the filming. Since Garry was one of the head writers, I wore a nice dress and high heels.

The audience sat in bleachers, like high schoolers at a football game, and when I arrived, Garry ushered me to a seat at the very top. I could hardly see the show. I never saw Garry during the filming, and he never introduced me to anyone.

As the audience was filing out at the end of the show, Garry met me in front of the bleachers. "So what did you think?" he asked.

"Why was I sitting up so high?"

"Joey doesn't like us to bring dates to the show," he said, "so I had to hide you up there. But what a great show, right?"

It turned out that Joey wanted everyone to think he wrote the show by himself, that all the jokes were his. He had an entire writing staff, but he made them hide behind the scenes. Garry was so young, hard-working, and grateful that he didn't put up a fuss. He was excited just to be living in Hollywood and writing for a television show.

When Garry wasn't working, he often was suffering from allergy attacks. He was allergic to a long list of condiments, including mustard, mayonnaise, vinegar, and horseradish, as well as many other foods. When I first met him, I didn't take his allergies that seriously. I knew he was a hypochondriac, and I thought he was exaggerating. That is, until I witnessed his first food-allergy attack.

Barbara, the nurse who had grown up in Glendale, invited us all over for a BBQ one Saturday. Just to be safe, I warned her about everything Garry was allergic to. I told her he was essentially allergic to every spicy ethnic dish under the sun, but that he loved ketchup and put it on everything. When she told me that she was making hamburgers, that seemed like a surefire, foolproof dish to keep Garry from getting sick. After all, he ate hamburgers all the time, smothering them in his beloved ketchup.

But I'd been wrong to think we were out of the culinary danger zone. Garry ate his hamburger and spent the rest of the night throwing up in the bathroom. I couldn't understand what had gone wrong. Barbara was perplexed, too.

"I don't understand it," she said. "I always mix my hamburgers with ice chips and a jar of mustard. Nothing else. Nothing fancy."

A jar of mustard? Mustard was at the top of the list of foods most dangerous to Garry's health. I had told Barbara, but she must not have heard me or hadn't quite believed me. I knew then and there that I would probably have to taste all Garry's food for the rest of my life. I soon became quite good at detecting even traces of mustard, mayonnaise, and vinegar.

As careful as I was, an allergy culprit would sometimes get by me.

That was the case at our friend Tommy's engagement party. First, as I often did, I went into the kitchen and discussed Garry's allergies with the catering staff. They showed me everything they were serving, and the chef assured me that everything was safe for Garry to eat. Later that evening, despite her assurances, Garry had trouble breathing.

It turned out the mini grilled cheese appetizers were laced with Worcestershire sauce. After that, I carried a syringe and a bottle of medicine in my purse. I knew what I was getting into, even if sometimes I felt like a private-duty nurse.

We dated through Thanksgiving and Christmas, but something changed at the big New Year's Eve party we went to. In the early 1960s in Los Angeles, it didn't seem people had long engagements or even engagement parties. Couples just talked about getting married for a few months and then went and did it, at least the people we knew. Most of us were transplants from other cities, with no family living locally. The weddings were usually small and attended mostly by new friends, with a reception in the basement of a church someplace in Hollywood or the San Fernando Valley.

Garry and I were getting the reputation among our friends as an established couple, and people were starting to ponder our future for us.

"You two make such a cute couple. When are you getting married?" someone asked us at the New Year's Eve party.

We artfully dodged the question. People continued to buzz about us, though, and by the end of the evening, the entire room had decided that Garry and I should pick a date and get married.

"How about January?" I said.

"July?" Garry asked.

"Too hot. February?" I offered.

"Maybe June," he suggested.

"No. I've got it. Let's do it in March on my birthday," I said. My birthday was March 9, which was also my father's birthday.

Everyone at the party cheered when we announced that we had

chosen a date. It was like a group decision. Unlike the last time I'd planned a wedding, there would be no invitations, no caterers, no lavish gifts to register for. I didn't even have an engagement ring, but it didn't bother me at all. We knew we didn't need all the bells and whistles. We just needed a bride, a groom, and a wedding date.

We decided that since our getting married had been a group decision, we should marry surrounded by our friends. We told everyone at the party that they were welcome to come if they paid their own way to Las Vegas. We chose to stay at the Sands Hotel. I asked Donna to be my maid of honor, and Garry asked Tommy to be his best man. That felt a little awkward, because they had broken up not long before, but they were still our best friends, and of course they agreed.

When we got married, Garry had $2,000 in his bank account, and I had no savings whatsoever. Donna and I still lived from week to week on our paychecks and bought bigger items on layaway. Except for the doctors at the hospital, who had careers, wives, and children, everyone we knew was living on a shoestring.

All my nursing friends except Peggy came to the wedding. One of us had to keep the intensive-care unit open, and Peggy drew the short straw, though she drove us to the airport. Many of Garry's friends were able to come as well. Unfortunately, we didn't have money to buy our families plane tickets, and they couldn't pay the airfare themselves. No one from either family came to our wedding.

Garry's dad blamed me, and my mom blamed Garry. My father and Garry's mother seemed content knowing that we were happy, and they didn't give us any grief. But his father and my mother could not get over the fact that their oldest children were getting married without them.

I remember the day I called to announce the good news. "Mom," I said. "I'm getting married on March 9th."

"Oh, really?" she said. "Who are you marrying?"

I told her about Garry, and that he was a writer.

"What does he write?" she asked.

"He writes for television," I said proudly.

"Television writers don't make any money. What happened to the doctor you were dating?"

"We broke up, Mom," I said.

"Too bad. So where are you getting married?"

"In Las Vegas," I said.

"Las Vegas?" she said. "Why would you want to get married there?"

"Mom, you just have to trust me. Garry is a wonderful man and he makes me laugh," I said. "We want a simple wedding. I just want you to be happy for me."

I knew I couldn't expect her to understand. She assumed I would want the kind of wedding I had planned with Jack. Nothing I said could convince her that my marriage to Garry wasn't about the actual wedding day but about spending the rest of our lives together.

To make matters worse, Garry was getting very anxious. The morning of the wedding, he was so green from nerves that my nursing friends gave him a get-well card and a bottle of a tonic to calm him down. Our wedding was set for three that afternoon in a Methodist church near the Sands, where we were all staying.

A few minutes before the wedding, the minister asked to speak to the two of us alone. We worried that he was going to ask us a series of difficult philosophical or theological questions. But all he wanted to know is why we had come all the way to Las Vegas to get married in a church. We told him it was because we wanted all our friends along for the celebration. And it was important to me to get married in a church, not a nondenominational chapel.

It was a very nice ceremony, and afterward we went back to the Sands and saw a dinner show with singer Patti Page. The waiter served us a cupcake with a candle in it to symbolize our wedding cake. We blew out the candle together and each made a wish. Joey Bishop paid for our hotel room.

Until then, we had lived in our separate apartments, mine in Barnsdall Terrace and his in Barnsdall Gardens. Supervising his building was a very nosy lady. If she so much as saw me walking with a shirt on a hangar near his apartment, she suspected some kind of

On March 9, 1963, in Las Vegas, outside the church at our wedding. Donna Palmer was my maid of honor and Tom Kuhn was Garry's best man.

cohabitation, and she would not stand for it. So Garry and I waited until after the wedding and then moved into a new apartment in Barnsdall Gardens.

CHAPTER THIRTEEN

WE GOT MARRIED ON March 9, 1963, and two weeks later, I found out I was pregnant. I worked at Cedars for the next three months, even though my battle with morning sickness made it difficult to get through a single day. One morning in the second week of July, I sat down on the couch in our apartment and couldn't stand up. That's when I realized that I could not continue working. I called the director of nursing and told her I was resigning, effective immediately.

I certainly hadn't planned to leave nursing so abruptly. In fact, I had three brand-new uniforms hanging in my closet. I promised that I would keep in touch with all my nursing friends, but it was time to say goodbye to my career and focus on my new family.

By September, my pregnancy was really starting to show. When the nosy building supervisor saw that I was pregnant, she said, "When will you be moving out? You know we don't allow children here."

Garry and I had already started looking for a new place. We found one on a street called Corning between Pico and Olympic, in a duplex that had been owned by a woman and her daughter. When the mother died, the daughter continued living in the upstairs unit and rented the downstairs apartment to us. It was furnished, so we moved right in and waited for the baby to arrive.

By mid-December, my physician, Dr. Melvin Ehrenhalt, said that I was due any day. On Christmas day, Garry was home from work when I felt labor pains begin. They were gentle, so we knew we had plenty of time, and I didn't mind when Garry said he had to run an errand. I learned later that he went to the home of his writing partner, Jerry Belson, where he'd stashed my Christmas present: a baby blue parakeet in a cage. When he got back, he snuck the bird into our apartment and hid it in a closet.

When Dr. Ehrenhalt examined me at the hospital, he said I was still many hours away from delivery. He knew we didn't have a lot of money, so he told us to go home and wait rather than paying for an extra night in the hospital. But I worried our apartment was too far away, so Garry suggested we visit his friend Fred Freeman, who lived on Rossmore, which was close to the hospital. Fred was heading out on a date and was reluctant to leave us in his apartment. He had just purchased a new couch and seemed worried I might go into labor and soil it. I sat in an old chair until Garry and I headed back to the hospital after midnight.

I didn't know any of the nurses in the maternity ward, and this side of Cedars was new to me. Before I was rolled into the delivery room, Dr. Ehrenhalt put the stethoscope on my belly and let Garry listen.

"It's the baby's heartbeat, Garry," he said.

Giving a hypochondriac a peek into a medical event is never a good idea. As Garry listened through the stethoscope, I could see him turning white as a ghost. Just looking at his anxious face was making me nervous, too.

"Garry, you look like you are going to pass out," I said. "You should go sit in the waiting room."

"Good idea," said the doctor.

Garry quickly complied and joined the other fathers-to-be in the waiting room, where he was much more comfortable smoking cigarettes and watching football on the television.

The birth of our first baby, on December 26, 1963, was not a difficult birth at all. She weighed a little over seven pounds, and we named her Lorraine Gay Marshall. Lorraine was my mother's middle name, and Gay was a nod to two of my best friends: Donna and Joan. We'd had a running joke about naming the baby after one of them, either Donna Kay or Joan Gail; then we decided to combine their middle names and give that to the baby for her middle name.

I put the baby in a bassinet by our bed, but she made little sounds through the night that kept Garry awake, so we moved her to a crib in her own room. Every time I fed her in the middle of the night,

On December 26, 1963, I gave birth to our first daughter, Lorraine Gay Marshall, who we would call Lori. This picture was taken outside our apartment on Corning Street.

though, I would get sleepy, so I started a new routine. I would take her into the living room and watch television while I nursed her. This worked well until the morning I woke up in my own bed, and when I went to look for the baby, she wasn't in her crib.

"I have lost the baby," I said to Garry.

"What do you mean you lost her?"

Lori was still in the living room, nestled beneath the coffee table, happy and safe. I think you make a lot of mistakes with your first child, but Lori was a very resilient baby. I was the first of my girlfriends to have a child, so we just incorporated her into our plans. We would take her to lunch, or shopping, or anywhere we needed to go. It would be a few years before they started having babies and Lori had other children to play with.

While I was home with the baby, Garry was beginning to build his reputation as a television writer, first with his partner Fred Freeman and later with Jerry Belson. In 1965, when *The Joey Bishop Show* was canceled after four seasons, he was hired to work on *The Danny*

Thomas Show. Sheldon Leonard and Danny Thomas were producing show after show, and it was a career-building step for Garry to become part of their team.

Some of the writers and their wives were invited to an anniversary party that Thomas and his wife, Rose Marie, hosted at Sportsmen's Lodge, in Studio City. Garry and I asked Donna to babysit. There I was, at a big Hollywood party, when I looked across the room and recognized someone. It made me giggle to think I knew someone at the party. The man was standing next to Sheldon Leonard, and I heard someone say he was married to Sheldon's daughter. I knew the man from a different situation: He had been a patient of mine in the intensive-care unit at Cedars. My hospital world was now colliding with my Hollywood world.

Garry also wrote for Lucille Ball. One of his best episodes for *The Lucy Show* was "Lucy and the Good Skate," in which she buys a pair of roller skates that are far too small, her feet swell up, and she has to wear the skates under her gown to a fancy event. I went to see the show filmed at Desilu Gower. I sat in the bleachers with Garry's mother, Marjorie, who was visiting from New York, and Lucy's mother, Desiree Hunt Ball. The two women had met at an earlier filming, and Desiree had invited Marjorie to join a group of Hollywood mothers of actors, producers, and writers. After the show wrapped, we went down onto the soundstage floor and met the cast and crew.

The only other time I met Lucy was at a beauty salon. I was going in for a facial and she was going in for some color. It was a Sunday afternoon, and I just gave her a little wave hello, as if we were acquaintances. The more often Garry worked in Hollywood, the more celebrities I met, but it never got old. To run into an actor or actress at a restaurant or a hair salon was always exciting. It seemed a million miles from the life I had left behind in Ohio, when I collected pop bottles to get enough change to buy a movie ticket.

When a script Garry had worked on was in production, he would work until 2 or 3 a.m. I would be home alone with the baby, and it made me a little nervous, so I set up a homemade security system:

a pyramid of soup cans by our front door. I figured if a burglar came through that door, he would knock over the cans, they would make a lot of noise, and he would run away. Of course, Garry came in that door, too.

"What the hell was all that noise?" he shouted one night. "What are these cans? What happened?!"

"I made my own burglar alarm," I said, quite proud of the system I had rigged up.

Garry remembered my soup-can pyramid when he was writing for *The Dick Van Dyke Show*. Most of the other writers were vying for scripts that centered on Dick, the star. Garry saw that if he could write scripts for Mary Tyler Moore, who played his wife, he could carve out his own niche. And that is what he did.

Garry didn't tell me he was stealing my idea; he just took it. One night when I was watching the show, I was shocked to see "Laura" creating a tower of soup cans while "Rob" is on a business trip.

"Hey, you can't just steal my ideas," I told Garry. "You should pay me something for them."

He agreed. He wouldn't tell me when and where he was using my material, but if I spotted something in a show that he'd taken from my life, he would pay me $25 in cash. In another episode, Laura is home alone taking a bath when she gets her toe stuck in the spout. Garry took this directly from an incident that happened to me. How often did Garry use material from my life? Let's just say that thanks to our agreement, I made a lot of walking-around money in the early and mid-1960s.

He was always writing late into the night. His desk was in our bedroom, so I had to teach myself to fall asleep to the sound of his fingers pecking away on the typewriter. Sometimes he would pace around the house, smoking cigarettes, and not sit down at the typewriter until after midnight.

"Why do you wait so late to get started?" I asked him one night.

"I don't have my thoughts together yet," he said.

Typically, Garry would give me $50 a week for the groceries. But when Garry and Jerry started doing freelance scripts for other shows, they would get paid in hundred-dollar bills, and he would surprise me with them. I would clear the dishes after dinner and discover a hundred-dollar bill under my plate. Or I would go to bed, and there would be one under my pillow. It became play money for us, because it was so unexpected, and always exciting to find.

One day, Donna and I took some of my cash and went to Saks Fifth Avenue, where fancy women shopped. We bought bathing suits, then we went to the shoe department and each selected a pair of elegant shoes. Donna liked a white pair, and I found a pair of patent-leather heels. When I went to pay for them, I handed the salesman two one-hundred-dollar bills. He took the money with a smirk.

"What?" I asked innocently.

"Wonder where you were last night," he said.

"What do you mean? I was home with my husband and baby."

"Really?" he said, still smirking. "Is that right? You didn't have a wild night?"

"No," I said. I had no idea what he was talking about. "What are you getting at?"

"The only women who pay in hundred-dollar bills are prostitutes," he said.

Donna and I were so shocked, we grabbed our shopping bags and left. When I got home from Saks, I told Garry, and he said to forget about it. Money was money, he said, and I shouldn't be embarrassed about paying in cash. We still didn't have a credit card, and the only way to buy anything was with cash, by check, or on layaway. The next time I went into a department store, I tried to hold my head high.

CHAPTER FOURTEEN

GARRY AND I GOT married so quickly, we did not meet each other's families until several months after the wedding. It wasn't that we didn't want to; they couldn't afford to come see us and we didn't have the money to fly them out to California.

In the summer of 1963, Garry had a job opportunity on the East Coast, and his parents picked us up at the airport in a big white sedan. His dad, Tony, was a bit of a showoff and liked to pretend he had more money than he did; his work in advertising was sometimes lucrative and sometimes not. The family had rented a few new houses during Garry's childhood, but for the most part, they lived in a modest apartment building in the Bronx. His mother, Marjorie, taught tap dancing in the basement, while her best friend, Mildred, made the costumes for the kids and collected money for the lessons from their parents.

The truth is, I didn't really care for Tony, but I thought Marjorie was terrific. I think Garry felt the same. Tony tried to be a big shot, but Marjorie was the talented one, performing and creating shows. Garry used to say she was the first director he ever met.

On the way home from the airport, we stopped for a "shore dinner." I had no idea what that was. It turned out to be lobster, a baked potato, and coleslaw. I had never had lobster in my life and wasn't sure how to eat it. Following his mother's lead, I used a shiny silver lobster cracker to break the shells but watched in amazement and distaste as she sucked the meat out of the claw. It was unlike any meal I had ever had. I wasn't that thrilled with it, but I was a few months' pregnant and could hardly eat anyway.

At their apartment, I met Marjorie's mother, who was blind. She was also named Marjorie, but they called her Nanny. She was a funny little lady who never spoke when Tony was around. The minute he left the apartment, however, Nanny would start talking, and talking, and usually say something bad about him.

"You know, Marjorie doesn't like him. He never gives her any money," Nanny told me. "Marjorie is trying to save up enough to leave him."

I didn't know how to respond to this, so I just listened as Nanny rambled on about what a bad guy Tony was.

Garry had been raised on live theater, so he was very excited to take me to see my first Broadway show, the musical *Oliver!* After our stay in New York, we flew to Chicago to visit his sister Ronny, her husband, and their two little girls. The day before we left, Marjorie called to give her a heads up.

"Don't bother buying any food for Barbara," Marjorie told her. "All she does is drink 7 Up and eat saltine crackers."

In Chicago, while Garry was having a beer with Ronny's husband, she confided a secret in me. "I want to leave my husband. I have about $14 in the bank, but I'm trying to save more."

So not only was Garry's mother plotting to leave his father, his sister was planning to leave her husband. It was quite an eye-opening trip. I just tried to be pleasant and not ruffle any feathers.

Later that summer, my entire family arrived on our doorstep. They had visited me twice before, but I hadn't known Garry then, and he didn't know what hit him. My mother had impulsively bought a new station wagon with air conditioning for the drive west. She had to do all the driving, because my dad didn't drive. On this trip, she drove to Tulsa, Oklahoma, and they spent a night with my grandmother. My mom's brother-in-law was a truck driver, and he gave her enough NoDoz to drive straight through to California. When she knocked on our front door, wired on NoDoz and coffee, she looked like the walking dead.

Garry and I were still in the small apartment in Barnsdall Gardens, so we paid for my family to stay in a motel around the corner. That first night, Garry invited Jerry Belson over to meet my parents. Garry thought he was terrible at small talk, but Belson knew how to chitchat, and he asked my parents about their drive, gas mileage, roadside diners, the weather, and the sights they'd seen along the way. He did all the talking while Garry sat in the corner, chain-smoking.

We took them to Disneyland and to dinner at Dino's Lodge, Dean Martin's restaurant on Sunset Boulevard. (By then, it had been sold, but it was still considered a hip, popular place.) My dad didn't have a sports jacket, which the restaurant required, so Garry loaned him one of his. Each day, my family would come over and make themselves at home. It felt cozy having them around, eating and watching television in our apartment, though I guess to Garry, it seemed like strangers were invading his domain.

By the following summer, we had moved into the duplex on Corning Street, and I convinced Garry to let my family stay with us. We had two bedrooms now, which seemed more than enough room. I thought it was fun having them there to play with the baby and me. One morning, Garry went into the living room, where my two brothers were asleep on the floor, as I was making breakfast for my parents, my sisters, and the baby. He got dressed and left the house, then called me from a nearby payphone.

"I'm not coming back for a while," he said.

"What are you talking about?"

"I'm not coming home until they are all gone," he said.

He hung up, and I telephoned Donna. I thought she would be the best person to analyze the situation.

"I think I have a problem," I told her. "My family is staying with us and Garry is not happy."

Garry agreed to meet us at a local diner. Donna offered support as I explained how important it was to me that my family stay with us, now that we had room. I always stayed with family members when I traveled, and that had meant bunking with lots of different people and making do. Donna, who had a family as big as mine, tried to explain the family dynamic to him. Then I tried to reason with him.

"Garry," I said, "it is only going to be a few more days, and then they will head off to my cousin's house in Santa Barbara. But you can't just stay away until they are gone. What would I tell them?"

In the summer of 1963, my family came to California and met my new husband for the first time. From left: Stephen, my mom and dad, me with Brenda, Garry, and Gloria.

He remained quiet.

"And besides, how much longer are my parents going to be alive, anyway? Shouldn't I see them as much as possible during these remaining years?"

Garry left for the bathroom and never came back to the table.

When we realized he wasn't coming back, Donna and I drove straight to Jerry Belson's house. I knew that's where Garry would be. Now I was crying, but I launched right back into my speech about how important my family was to me.

"I don't understand how you can be this way," I said. "This is my family, and family is supposed to stay with you."

I hammered at Garry for so long, he finally said okay, my family could stay with us. "But do they have to come every year?" he asked.

"Maybe," I said. "But I'm not going to let this ruin our marriage."

By the next year, my brother Jimmy had joined the Navy, and the family consisted of a smaller group. But they continued to come to

California each year, and I think eventually Garry grew to like them.

The irony is that over the next few years, we saw much less of my family and much more of his. In the late '60s, Garry's mother moved to Los Angeles, saying it was to get away from his dad. Tony grew jealous of the attention Marjorie was getting, so he moved here, too. Then his sister Penny moved to Los Angeles with her baby, and soon after that, Ronny left her husband in Chicago and moved to California with her three girls. Marjorie expected Garry to get everyone a job on his television shows.

I think Garry and Jerry Belson still hold the record for most freelance television scripts written in one year, which is more than 35. So it was not completely out of the blue when, in 1965 or 1966, producer Lee Rich offered them a chance to write and produce their own TV show. They developed a half-hour sit-com called *Hey, Landlord*, about a group of young people who live in their friend's brownstone apartment building in Manhattan.

Hey, Landlord was on NBC, a three-camera show with a live audience. I took a few girlfriends to watch the filming of the pilot episode. We found our seats in the bleachers and waited for the curtain below to be pulled back and reveal the set. While we were waiting, my friend Barbara Hauptman began having a terrible allergy attack.

"What's wrong, Barbara. What can I do?" I asked.

"I don't know. The only thing I'm allergic to is horses," she said. "There couldn't possibly be a horse down there on that soundstage, could there?"

"Of course not," I said.

A few minutes later, the curtain opened, and there was an actress with the long hair of Lady Godiva sitting on a white horse.

Even though the show had a good cast and a great time slot—on Sunday evenings right after *Walt Disney's Wonderful World of Color* and before *Bonanza*—it couldn't compete against *The Ed Sullivan Show*, on CBS, and was canceled after only one season. Despite the show's lack of success, it proved that Garry was capable not only of writing comedy but of producing his own show. He also directed an episode.

CHAPTER FIFTEEN

AFTER LORI WAS BORN, we tried for several years to get pregnant but were unsuccessful. Fertility treatments were not yet an option. Our OB-GYN worked with a pediatrician who had a brother who was a lawyer, and the three of them set up legal adoptions. Garry and I were just starting to think about that when my doctor suggested we go on vacation, try to relax, and forget about trying to get pregnant for a while. We went to England and Ireland and had a wonderful time. When I saw Buckingham Palace, I remembered how much I'd enjoyed writing my eighth-grade report on Queen Elizabeth, and how long I had dreamed of seeing cities like London and Dublin.

After Lori was born, I had trouble getting pregnant again. My doctor suggested a vacation might help. In 1967, Garry and I dropped Lori off in Ohio to stay with my parents and headed to London and Dublin for the first time.

On the flight home, I did not feel well and thought it might be morning sickness. We were so optimistic, we even started discussing baby names. I said I liked the name Kathleen; I had always loved Katharine Hepburn but thought the name Kathleen had a sweeter ring. Garry liked that name, too. My middle name is Sue. I told Garry I would have preferred the more elegant Susan, and we chose that for the middle name, if I was pregnant and we had a girl. When we got back to L.A., I went to the doctor as soon as I could and found our relaxing vacation had done the trick.

Early in the pregnancy, we spent an evening with Debbie Reynolds, which was a big deal for me. Garry and Jerry Belson were branching out into movie scripts, and Garry had met with her about a screenplay they'd written called *How Sweet It Is!* He thought she would be great in the lead. After their meeting, Debbie invited us to her beautiful house in Beverly Hills, where she lived with her then-husband Harry Karl.

I was so impressed that there were oil paintings on the walls. I thought it was the kind of art you might find in a museum. Growing up, I'd certainly never seen any artwork in any house I visited in Ohio or Kentucky.

We sat down to a formal dinner in the dining room, and I remember noticing a button on the floor near Debbie's chair. She was supposed to press it gently with her foot to call the waiter. For some reason, the button wasn't working that night, so Debbie pounded her foot on the floor. That gave us all the giggles, and when the waiter finally came out of the kitchen, it was to see why we were laughing so hard.

Debbie did sign on to star in *How Sweet It Is!*, opposite James Garner. As the screenwriters, Garry and Jerry got to visit the set, sometimes to punch up parts of the script. Some of the scenes took place on a cruise ship, and Garry was looking forward to joining the crew on the water. By this time, however, I was far along in my pregnancy. In those days, it was more difficult to predict when a baby would arrive, so Garry stayed on dry land with me. Our second daughter, Kathleen Susan Marshall, was born on December 16, 1967, and the movie came out the following summer.

After Kathleen was born, I quickly got pregnant again. I started to worry that my third child would be a boy and that everyone, especially Garry's dad, would make such a fuss over him, it would overshadow Kathleen's childhood. I just wanted healthy, happy children. When I gave birth to our son, Scott Anthony Marshall, on January 17, 1969, my hospital room was filled with the sports toys and other boy-themed gifts that Garry's friends and co-workers had sent. When I saw them, I started to cry.

"What's the matter?" Garry asked. "You should be happy. We have a boy."

"I am happy. I just don't want you to forget that we had a little girl just over a year ago," I said.

Garry promised me he had enough love and time to devote to all three of our children, and he never let them down. They became part of the fabric of Garry's home and work life. In fact, with each new project, whether a movie or a television show, he had me bring the kids to the set. Sometimes they even got work as extras.

The summer after Scott was born, *The Grasshopper*, a movie Garry and Jerry had worked on, starring Jacqueline Bisset, the football player Jim Brown, and Joseph Cotten, was shooting in Las Vegas. Scott got a small part playing a baby. It was so hot, and in those days, the child-labor laws weren't very strict. He filmed his scene over the course of two long days, with breaks for naps. Every time he woke up from a nap, he started screaming. Eventually, we were finally able to finish his scene and go home.

By now, we were living in Toluca Lake, a small, leafy neighborhood situated between Burbank, Studio City, and North Hollywood. Our friends Dave and Louise Ketchum lived there with their daughter, Nikki, who was Lori's age. Garry and I had visited them one day when Lori was about two and a half. We walked around the neighborhood and found it to be pristine and lovely, very quiet and green. Garry liked its wide sidewalks, which he felt a proper family neighborhood should have. It had a suburban feel, but there were restaurants and shops nearby. We picked up the phone and called a realtor.

While Garry and Jerry's screenplay writing did not immediately lead to more film work, their offers for television scripts had skyrocketed. Garry was starting to work at different studios, and his goal in life was to never have to get on the freeway. He was just not a good enough driver to use the on- and off-ramps, with all those other cars speeding by. It had taken him three tries to get his driver's license in the first place. A major reason we bought a house in Toluca Lake was because he could take surface streets to most of the big studios, including Warner Brothers and Paramount.

Another big reason was Paty's, a restaurant on Riverside Drive that is still there today. Not only was Paty's open 24 hours a day, it also had a cigarette machine. If Garry was up late writing and he ran out of cigarettes, he could easily drive or even walk to Paty's with some change in his pocket and buy more.

We soon found a ranch-style house at 4405 Arcola Avenue, right on the corner. It was listed for something like $35,000. Interest rates were very low, and our accountant advised us to get a fixed-rate mortgage to make sure interest on the loan would not go up for five years. That turned out to be excellent advice, especially for new homeowners like us. Garry, of course, turned green when we signed the loan papers, even though he had a steady income.

When we moved in, we had hardly any furniture: a king-size bed, a rocking chair, a bed for the baby. We saved S&H Green Stamps and bought Lori a tricycle, which she rode around our empty living room. We bought a card table to eat on, and then a refrigerator and a washer and dryer. We lived in that house for the next eight years, as our family grew from three to five. Lori and Kathleen shared a bedroom and Scott had his own room.

We met a nice family across the street, the Weisburds, whose three children were almost exactly the same ages as ours. They had a swimming pool, and in the summer, we spent nearly every day with them. Bob Hope and his wife, who also lived across the street, had half a golf course on their land. We rarely saw them, but it was fun saying we lived across the street from them. The kids, however, did not appreciate the year his staff handed out headshots of Hope instead of Halloween candy. They would have preferred chocolate.

I enjoyed giving dinner parties in our new house. Often, we'd invite some of Garry's colleagues, such as Carl Reiner and his wife, Estelle. When our children were little, they would come out in their pajamas during cocktail hour and say hello to our guests; then I would put them to bed and serve dinner. I would make things from *Joy of Cooking*, such as Waldorf salad, split pea soup (Garry's favorite), and beef stroganoff. I liked serving filet mignon, because you didn't have to cook it long for it to be a crowd pleaser.

I was able to find a supermarket that delivered, but otherwise I was doing all the cooking, cleaning, and childcare. I thought I was doing okay until one night when Garry came home from a late-night writer's table at 2 a.m. The washer and dryer were on, and I was sitting in the middle of the kitchen floor, a mop in my hand, fast asleep.

"Barbara," he said, "we need to get some help."

I reached for the phonebook and found an advertisement that read "24-hour-a-day cleaning service." The man who answered said I should come to his office, on Santa Monica Boulevard in Beverly Hills, the next day to meet a housekeeper he had in mind. The next day, I met Maria Tellez, who had recently moved to Los Angeles from Texas. When I brought her home to meet the kids, she immediately started making their beds. I thought she was fabulous. She stayed with us for the next 25 years. Maria was family.

While Garry was very supportive of my getting cleaning and childcare help, he was not as happy when I hired an interior decorator. Her name was Lil Chain, and Garry acted as if she were Cruella De Vil, out to steal his wallet and take all his money. Having grown up in a small apartment in the Bronx, Garry had never met an interior decorator. He went to a showroom with Lil once to look at some fabric, and the experience terrified him so much, he would never go back. I told him that decorating the house was going to be up to me, and he should let me take the lead.

Since we were both frugal people, he had to trust me when I said I would not go overboard.

The first thing we bought through the decorator was a blue-fabric couch, paired with blue-and-green rattan furniture. Lil brought us a decorative cat with blue writing on it for the den. When Garry saw it sitting on the mantel, he made a face.

"What's wrong?" I asked.

"I don't like cats," he said.

"But it is ceramic," I said. "It certainly won't scratch you."

I sent the cat back anyway. The next thing Lil brought us was a candy dish, and Garry went through the roof.

"Are you kidding me? Fourteen dollars for a candy dish?!" After that, I started hiding the bills from him. It was better if he learned to appreciate the decor without knowing what it cost.

Lil papered our den with illustrated wallpaper, an Italian scene with a fountain. I thought it was beautiful; Garry much preferred the living room, which was still empty except for a ping-pong table and a pinball machine. But the reality was he was making more money, and it was okay to spend some of it decorating our first house. It just took him a long time to reach that conclusion.

CHAPTER SIXTEEN

MANY MOMENTS IN GARRY'S career stand out to me as pivotal, and probably the first is when he and Jerry Belson were hired by Paramount to develop a television version of Neil Simon's hit play *The Odd Couple* for ABC. The play, which originally starred Art Carney and Walter Matthau, opened in 1965 and closed after almost a thousand performances. The story centers on the relationship of two mismatched men after Felix, neurotic and fastidious, moves in with his friend Oscar, a slovenly sportswriter. Matthau, who won a Tony for his performance, also played Oscar in the 1968 film version. Jack Lemmon played Felix.

Garry would be executive producer as well, which meant that his status changed from writer to "show runner." I knew this would mean longer hours and more stress for him, but it was also a big step forward and would eventually bring more money for our family. We really had no idea how far his career would go. We just knew that producing the television version of this hit play and film was exciting.

In the late 1960s, the Paramount lot was dead. No other shows were being filmed, and both Paramount and ABC were hopeful that *The Odd Couple* would be a hit. Tony Randall was already attached to the show as Felix Unger. Jack Klugman had played Oscar Madison after Matthau for a few months, and Garry had seen him in *Gypsy* opposite Ethel Merman and thought he was terrific. When he asked Paramount to get Klugman to audition, they sent an actor with a black mustache whose name was Jack Kruschen. Garry yelled, "Kruschen? I said "Klugman!" Eventually, the right Jack was found and hired and went on to win two Emmy Awards and a Golden Globe for his portrayal of Oscar. Randall also won an Emmy for his work on this show.

We got to know Jack, his actress wife, Brett Somers, and his two sons; Jack remained one of Garry's closest friends for the next 40 years. We grew close to Tony as well but rarely saw his wife, Florence, because she lived in New York. I remember having dinner at the Brown Derby with them once, and Florence, who seemed older than Tony, didn't appear to like the Hollywood life. Jack and Brett, on the other hand, were the toast of the town both before and after they divorced.

When work on *The Odd Couple* began, in 1970, Garry's sister Penny was sleeping on our couch. She had been married briefly in New Mexico and had a baby girl; when the marriage didn't work out, she moved to L.A. By then, her parents were living here. Every day, Garry's mother would call and say, "Could you please give Penny a job?!" I was supportive of any plan that would get her off our couch. And that is how Penny became Oscar Madison's secretary, Myrna Turner, on *The Odd Couple.*

One problem was a rumor we heard that Neil Simon was not happy about the show. The rumor turned out to be true, but it had nothing to do with Garry and Jerry. According to Garry, Neil got a bad buyout deal from Paramount. Years later, he told Garry that when his daughter became a fan of the show, she made him watch it, and he liked it. But we didn't find that out for a long time. All we knew was that Neil Simon was not a fan of the show, and while that didn't stop it from moving forward, it was a little uncomfortable to think he didn't approve.

Producing *The Odd Couple* was an incredible responsibility. Garry was very stressed most of the time, and he began smoking more. I noticed that sometimes he would race through dinner with the children just so he could get to his after-dinner cigarette. When he was writing at home, he would chain-smoke all night, lighting his new cigarette from the old one. He wanted *The Odd Couple* to be a success both in the ratings and with the critics, and he put most of the pressure on himself.

During those years, I felt slightly adrift. I knew a lot of Hollywood wives who liked to shop, but I really wasn't one of them. I had too much to do at home to go back to nursing. But sometimes I would be at the supermarket and think, "I have more energy than this. There must be something else I can do while the kids are at school." As Lori and then Kathi and Scott started preschool at nearby Valley Campus School, I started looking for something else to do.

I met Belle Dubnoff, a psychologist, at a dinner party. She was using her own backyard to educate young children with special needs, who were not getting enough support from the public-school system. She created educational material for each child. When we met, she was trying to raise money to move the school into its own building, which she would call the Dubnoff Center for Child Development, and that inspired me to join a group of women who were helping her. I started going to meetings with these women, many of whom were also married to men in the entertainment industry.

One year, we decided to put on a fundraising fashion show, asking movie stars and their children to be our models. Garry and Jerry agreed to write a script, and Saks supplied the clothing. Our models included Frances Bergen and her daughter, Candice, and son, Kris; Debbie Reynolds and her daughter, Carrie Fisher; and Shirley Jones and several of her little boys. Steve McQueen's wife, actress and dancer Neile Adams, was also a model for us. I thought McQueen was very overprotective; he didn't want her out of his sight for a minute.

We worked with Saks to dress the mothers and children in coordinating outfits. Carrie, who was probably 12 or 13 years old, got very pissy and refused to come out of her dressing room. Debbie was so mad at her and forced her to do it, and she came down the runway with a pout on her face.

We dubbed the show *Moms and Moppets* and put it on for years. Garry and Jerry continued to write the scripts, but every year they were so busy, they waited until the last minute. One year when they started writing at midnight, I was beyond nervous. But they always came through and filled the fashion show with many laughs.

Garry was so busy that I had to carve out private time with him. Our annual family Easter vacation to Carmel was the only trip he would commit to, although he would be penciling up *Odd Couple* scripts while I did all the driving. While we never had time to go to Las Vegas or Palm Springs anymore, I could get him to agree to an occasional getaway to Newport Beach. The two of us would leave on a Friday night and drive straight there. In those days, there was a television channel that showed old movies on Monday mornings. I convinced him that he could sleep in, watch the Monday-morning movie, and still make it to *The Odd Couple* table reading that afternoon.

In those years, as you can imagine, the kids didn't see their dad much. He would be sleeping when they left for school, and they would be asleep when he came home from the studio late at night. I had to find ways to help the kids stay connected to him. Sometimes I would leave my two little ones at home with Maria and drive Lori down to Paramount to have dinner with Garry. We would eat at Nickodell, on Melrose just outside the Paramount gate, then he would return to the set and we would drive home.

Later, when Garry wanted Lori to see what he did for a living, he cast her in an episode of *The Odd Couple*. At first, Lori wanted nothing to do with the show, because she'd heard that Tony Randall didn't like children. That was only partially true: Tony didn't want children in the audience while the show was being filmed, because he thought they would be a distraction. He was fine with Lori being in the show.

Lori was taking piano lessons from a very serious Frenchwoman named Ms. Pierre, who also ran our local preschool, and Garry wanted Lori to play Mendelssohn's "Wedding March." I asked Ms. Pierre if she could teach Lori that piece, and then invited her to come watch the episode (it was called "Welcome to the Army, Mr. Madison") being filmed. What I didn't know is that Garry had taught Lori how to play the "Wedding March" very badly, to make the scene funnier.

The studio audience roared with laughter during that scene, but Ms. Pierre did not laugh at all. She was baffled by Lori's playing. "She knows how to play it perfectly! I don't understand!" she kept

I gave birth to Kathleen Susan Marshall in 1967 and Scott Anthony Marshall in 1969; they were just 13 months apart. With three children in the family now, we found a larger house, still in Toluca Lake.

By the late 1960s, Garry's whole family had moved to Los Angeles. We often had them over for barbecues. Here, at our home on Arcola Avenue, his sisters Ronny (left) and Penny are in the back row with us. In the middle row are his parents and Nanny. In the front row, with all the cousins, is our beloved housekeeper, Maria Tellez, on the far right.

saying. It was one of the many times I had to explain that sometimes Garry did things because they were funny, not because they were correct.

The Odd Couple marked the transformation of Garry from a staff writer into a boss. The studio and the network were not happy if you were the boss of a single show, however; they wanted you to create more shows. I remember the day Garry came home from a meeting with the head of Paramount Pictures, Michael Eisner.

"How did it go?" I asked.

"Eisner wants me to create a new TV show," Garry said.

"About what?" I asked.

"A Swedish family in the 1930s. Like *I Remember Mama*."

"But you don't know anything about Sweden or the 1930s," I said.

"Exactly. That's what I told him. I convinced him to let me make a pilot about a family in Milwaukee in the 1950s," he said.

And that is how *Happy Days* was born. Jerry Belson had no interest in the new show, so after more than ten years of working together, they agreed to stay friends but part ways as writing and producing partners. What none of us knew when Garry embarked alone on this show is that it would change our lives.

CHAPTER SEVENTEEN

AS GARRY WROTE IN his two memoirs and said often in press interviews and speaking engagements, the *Happy Days* set was a wonderful place to work during its 11-season run. He rarely shared with the public the fact that he hardly paid attention to the show during its first season. He was too busy running the final season of *The Odd Couple*, which was always considered a more intellectual and critically acclaimed show. The fact that *Happy Days* became a longer running and more lucrative hit was, I think, a complete surprise and ultimately a great joy for Garry.

Happy Days was more like the Danny Thomas shows that Garry had started out writing for. It was a family show, where nobody swore or made fun of one another; everyone got along. Its trip to prime time, however, was anything but smooth. The pilot, in which former child actor Ron Howard plays the teenage son of a family that buys its first TV set, didn't sell; so Garry sold it as a one-off episode to *Love American Style*, which titled it "Love and the Television Set." The pilot sat on the shelf until 1973, when George Lucas released his film *American Graffiti* and everyone was excited about the '50s again. (Lucas had even screened the episode to watch Ron Howard's performance.) Thanks to the success of *American Graffiti*, Eisner decided the 1950s was indeed a good decade in which to set a show, and he gave Garry the green light to bring it back to life.

The cast members of *Happy Days* really did consider themselves family. As the mother and father of Richie Cunningham (Howard) and his siblings, Marion Ross and Tom Bosley were the wise and nurturing parents of the group. The show focused at first on Richie and two of his friends, played by Anson Williams and Don Most, until Arthur "Fonzie" Fonzarelli (Henry Winkler), a secondary character, became a fan favorite, and his role was expanded. Howard and Winkler were both dating women they would marry, but during the first few seasons, it was mostly a set of single young actors, grateful to have a steady paycheck and supportive co-stars.

Before she moved to Los Angeles, Marjorie, Garry's mother, would come from New York for long visits. In those days, I would often get a sitter and we would go to dinner at Farmers Market, with its shops and restaurants, at Third and Fairfax and then watch a live taping of *The Carol Burnett Show* at CBS. Carol was Marjorie's absolute favorite performer; she couldn't get enough of her. But once Garry created *Happy Days*, we started going to see it being filmed.

When the show took off, no one was more surprised than Garry. The higher the ratings, the more money the cast and producers made, and the more power Garry developed. Garry was quite clear with the cast about how he would use that power.

"If you want a better parking spot on the lot, or a nicer lamp in your dressing room, don't come to me," he would say. "But if you want a better joke, or aren't happy with your story line, then I'm the guy to come talk to."

Everyone on the set knew I was a nurse. Cast and crew members often came to me with their aches and ailments. And even though I had retired to raise my family, nursing was never far from my mind. I maintained my credentials year after year. In the 1960s and '70s, you didn't need to take additional classes to do that; you simply had to pay a renewal fee. In the late '70s, however, the National Registered Nursing Association decided that nurses had to take 30 hours of instruction every three years to keep their licenses. I usually took one-day, seven-hour classes, covering subjects such as new drugs and new treatments, to maintain my nursing license.

One night, Garry got a call from Jerry Belson, who told him Harvey Miller, another writer friend, was standing on an apartment balcony threatening to jump. Jerry thought I might be able to calm Harvey down, but I wasn't going to mess around with a suicidal comedy writer who was probably on drugs. I told Jerry to call 911, and I guess the emergency medics were able to get Harvey down, because he lived another 30 years.

Many of the people I met in Hollywood, unlike those I'd known growing up in Ohio, bordered on the eccentric, to say the least. They had access to plenty of money and plenty of drugs. I never went through a drug period myself, so it was difficult for me to understand all the craziness that was going on. Once, a famous television actress and friend took LSD and telephoned Garry and me for help. We knew she liked doing crossword puzzles, so Garry and I talked to her while she did one and eventually came down from her high.

So many of Garry's friends were in show business that I stood out, the lone nurse among a sea of writers, actors, directors, and producers. Garry used to have a Saturday basketball game at our house, and one Saturday one of the guys brought along his girlfriend, a well-known actress. While the guys were playing basketball, she asked to use my telephone. She spent the rest of the day lying on my bed and talking to her niece, who was having some kind of psychiatric breakdown. For weeks after that, the actress would call me for advice on her niece's care. She liked talking to me, she said, because I was the only nurse she knew in Hollywood.

In the 1980s, Garry and I went each year to La Costa Resort, near San Diego, for a celebrity tennis tournament. Estelle and Carl Reiner and Anne Bancroft and her husband, Mel Brooks, went, too. Clockwise from top left: Garry, Anne, Mel, Carl, and producer and writer Norman Lear.

Garry and I often went to La Costa Resort, in Carlsbad, just north of San Diego, because it was easy to get a babysitter and drive down for the weekend. One weekend, we were there for a celebrity tennis tournament that took place each year. One of the highlights was a talent show put on by the men. Every year, two of Garry's colleagues, Mel Brooks and Carl Reiner, attended the tournament with their wives, Anne Bancroft and Estelle Reiner, and this particular year, the two decided that the talent show should no longer be men only. They wanted all the women to perform, too.

In 1984, Garry and I performed in the talent show at the La Costa tennis tournament. He told jokes while I put an Ace bandage on his arm as a band behind us played faster and faster. The crowd roared.

I was horrified. The last time I had performed in a talent show, I'd been in nursing school, and it was a far cry from Hollywood standards. But Anne and Estelle insisted that if the men were going to perform, the women were, too. Garry had an idea for a bit that we could do together, and he wanted to surprise me with it onstage. I couldn't imagine what I could do to make these famous people laugh. But I trusted Garry and his great comedic timing.

"Anne and Estelle were terrific," Garry told the crowd after they performed. "But now I'm going to introduce you to my wife, Barbara, and I think you will find her quite interesting. She is a nurse, and I'm going to show you what she can do."

He took an Ace elastic bandage out of his pocket, handed it to me, and asked me to put the bandage on his arm. While I did this, he told a funny story as a band behind us played. Garry's delivery, coupled with my no-nonsense bandaging of his arm to musical accompaniment, made the audience roar. The music kept getting faster and faster as I wrapped the bandage and he told jokes. People were falling out of their seats. That was one of the few times I performed onstage, but it was memorable. People at the La Costa tennis tournament were still talking about it ten years later.

Because I was a nurse, I was often asked to join my children's school field trips. Most of the time, I was an extra chaperone. But one year, when I accompanied a group to Yosemite, we were blindsided by a flu epidemic. I had to take care of 21 sick students and two sick teachers. The group was too ill to send home, so we moved out of log cabins and into hotel rooms. I went to the cafeteria every day and got hot water to make them all instant chicken noodle soup. For a solid week, day and night, I fielded high fevers, vomiting, and phone calls from nervous parents. The following year, the school invited me back, and I finally got to see what Yosemite was like.

I loved being able to call myself a nurse. It meant that I could help people, and that seemed to comfort them as well as me. One of the things you have to know about Garry is that he'd been a very sick little boy. Allergic to dozens of foods and pollens, he spent most of his childhood in and out of bed. The sad thing is that he wanted to be a baseball star like Joe DiMaggio, and being sickly did not fit well with that dream. He sneezed and wheezed and got hurt so often that his grandmother once said she'd give him a dollar if he stopped bleeding.

Somehow, Garry managed to survive childhood, make it into adulthood, and meet me. I was very protective of Garry's health. If we were invited to a dinner party, I would always call ahead and make sure the hostess was aware of Garry's allergies to common foods like mustard and horseradish. If we were in a restaurant, I would often taste Garry's food first, like a member of the royal court testing a king's dish for traces of poison. Food allergies were one thing—more than anything else, I had to constantly monitor Garry for signs of stress, anxiety, and exhaustion.

Garry was not after power or fame; he wanted to make people laugh. He liked working, and the more he worked, the more the studio and the network gave him to do. I think if he'd had only *Happy Days* on the air, we might have had a nice quiet life. But a series of spinoffs followed, and the success of these shows affected not only the course of Garry's career but also his health, our marriage, and our life with the children.

CHAPTER EIGHTEEN

GARRY'S STRESS LEVEL ON *The Odd Couple* and *Happy Days* was relatively low. He had an incredible amount of responsibility, but also loyal writers and producers, as well as calm, dedicated actors. *Laverne & Shirley*, however, was an entirely different experience.

Garry had cast Penny in *The Odd Couple* because she needed a job. Both Tony Randall and Jack Klugman were very nurturing and took the time to teach her about acting. Once *The Odd Couple* ended, in 1975, she needed another show. Garry had an epiphany that kept his sister employed.

In 1999, we celebrated a reunion of The Odd Couple *with Heather and Tony Randall and Jack and Peggy Klugman. I still remain friends with Peggy and Heather.*

"I don't see many blue-collar women on television," he told the network. As Laverne DeFazio and Shirley Feeney, Penny and Cindy Williams had appeared in an episode of *Happy Days* as friends of Fonzie's, girls from "the wrong side of the tracks" who work in a brewery. Garry got the money to shoot a pilot—in the middle of the night, using our daughters' stuffed animals as props, because there wasn't even a set—and in 1976 *Laverne & Shirley* became a series almost like magic. It did feel exciting, almost as if Garry had a Midas touch with television. But things turned unpleasant rather quickly.

I was not thrilled when *Laverne & Shirley* sold, because I could tell that Garry was already running on empty. Then the cast began to demand more and more of his time. He began to eat badly and often had to take Maalox and Pepto-Bismol to calm his stomach. He began having anxiety attacks; his breathing would become heavy and he would start to hyperventilate. He often went to Nickodell, the restaurant outside Paramount, before the shows filmed, again in front of a live audience. When Garry's favorite waitress saw him start to breathe like that, she would quickly get him a paper bag. He would breathe deeply into the bag until he had calmed himself down.

Garry also had less and less time for the kids and me. Family had always been a priority for him, but when someone in the cast called him, screaming, he always drove back to the studio and addressed their needs. One night when we were all eating dinner at the kitchen table, I looked out the window and saw Penny climbing over our locked gate, the latest script wedged under her arm. Garry never said no to his sister. He was very protective of Penny and always thought he could solve her troubles with a better line or a joke.

Garry was a writer first and foremost, and he would stay up later than anyone on a show to make a script better. Penny and Cindy, however, did not treat the show's writers well. They would chew them up and spit them out, sending the writers running to Garry and handing in their resignations. The staff turnover was so high that Garry started begging writers and producers from *Happy Days* to come work on the new show. One of the producers was Arthur Silver, a very patient and lovely man. Garry convinced him to try his hand at fixing *Laverne & Shirley*. After just one week, Arthur was begging Garry to let him go back to *Happy Days*.

"What happened, Arthur?" Garry asked. "Please tell me. I want to know."

"I got into my car. I started to pull out of my parking space. I looked up and saw Penny and Cindy walking across the lot, and suddenly I had the urge to step on the gas pedal. For the first time in my life, I wanted to run two people down with my car. I can't work like this, Garry. It is too stressful," said Arthur. Garry, of course, immediately sent Arthur back to the safety of the *Happy Days* soundstage.

The children and I shook our heads in amazement at the time and energy it took to produce the show. Garry said the children could come on the set of *Happy Days* anytime they wanted, but they could never visit *Laverne & Shirley*, he told me, because there was "too much fighting and swearing going on."

During the *Laverne & Shirley* years, Garry was smoking more and more, up to two packs a day, and getting thinner and thinner. We consulted a doctor, who suggested high-calorie, high-energy shakes to boost Garry's weight and strength. But the more he worked, the harder Paramount and the network pushed him. Finally, I had to take matters into my own hands. I decided that Garry should move off the Paramount lot and rent some office space in the Valley, closer to home.

Michael Eisner was in Switzerland skiing when he heard Garry was moving off the lot. When Eisner called our home to discuss it with him, I answered the phone.

"Barbara," he said, "I heard a rumor that Garry is moving off the Paramount lot."

"He can't stand to be on the same lot as his sister. He is a nervous wreck, and it is not healthy for him. He is smoking too much, eating badly, and losing weight. He hyperventilated into a paper bag the other night at the Nickodell, and our children were mortified. He needs his own office, away from Paramount."

"How much money will it take to keep him on the lot?" Eisner asked.

"This is not about money, Michael," I said. People in Hollywood always think the bottom line is money. I was trying to protect my husband's health and sanity.

"I'll build him a new wing, or a new building, across the lot. He can even have his own entrance," he said. "Penny will never see him coming and going."

Suddenly I felt like a Hollywood agent negotiating a big deal for my client.

"Michael, it is not about giving him more things; it is about giving him a calm and safe space so he can do his work," I said. "We both know how talented Garry is, but he cannot be creative any longer if he stays on the Paramount lot."

We moved Garry into an apartment building on Tujunga Avenue near Ventura Boulevard. It had a pool and easy parking and was a five-minute drive from our home. However, the apartment manager didn't allow businesses to be based there, so we had to pretend one of Garry's secretaries lived in the apartment. She brought over some of her clothing, a bathrobe, even a puzzle to leave out on the table to give it that lived-in look.

Garry wanted his children to watch his television shows, and when he noticed that Scott was not watching *Happy Days*, he asked why. Scott said it was because there were no space aliens. That's how Garry invented Mork from Ork, who, portrayed by Robin Williams, made a memorable appearance on the show. In 1978, Garry went on to create *Mork & Mindy*, with Williams and Pam Dawber—another spinoff from *Happy Days*. At one point, all three of Garry's shows were at the top of the Nielsen ratings. He was very proud of that achievement.

He would go on to create *Joanie Loves Chachi*, *Angie*, *Blansky's Beauties*, and pilots that went into production but never sold like the other ones did. None of these shows got the critical acclaim of *The Odd Couple*, but that didn't matter, because they made people laugh and made money for the network and studio. Garry used to say, "If television is the education of America, then I am recess." He began to make a lot of money from mastering recess.

By then, Garry had hired his sister Ronny to work on his television shows. Ronny, who preferred to work behind the camera, started as an associate producer and eventually became an executive producer on shows like *Happy Days*, *Laverne & Shirley*, *Joanie Loves Chachi*, and *Blansky's Beauties*. It made Garry very happy to have both his sisters in California.

Despite the popular and financial success of his television shows, Garry continued to lose weight and was exhausted all the time. We took short trips to Carmel with the children and to Newport Beach by ourselves, but I started to search for other ways for Garry to relax. Our friends Dave and Louise Ketchum had recently purchased a mobile home. I imagined it would be fun to travel with our own accommodations rather than stay in motels. I dreamed of driving our own mobile home across the country, exploring the southern U.S. and then heading to Cincinnati to be with my family.

Before we made a commitment to buying a mobile home, I thought we should rent one and test-drive it on a trip. The Ketchums agreed to join us, and we caravanned to Santa Barbara.

I made a reservation at a mobile-home park, and when we pulled in, the kids jumped out of the car and Garry started to follow them, as if he were one of the children, too.

"What are you doing?" I said, kind of stomping my feet to get his attention before he headed for the playground.

"Going to play in the park with the kids," he said.

"I can't do all of this alone," I said.

"Do what?"

"We have to hook up the plumbing and electricity for the camper," I said.

There was a long pause as this knowledge sank in.

"I think maybe this is not for us," Garry said. "Maybe we are hotel people after all."

And he was right. The mobile-home experience was a bust from the beginning. I realized we really liked staying in hotels. In 1975, we went to the East Coast. I thought that would be a great way to show the kids cities like Boston in the year before the Bicentennial. Visiting tourist attractions throughout Massachusetts was a breeze.

The next year, we took the kids to Victoria and Vancouver, British Columbia, and that was a successful trip, too. Garry and I took trips to San Francisco with our friends Ruth and Jerry Paris to see Rams football games, stay at the Mark Hopkins, and eat at the Tadich Grill.

Traveling for us was not a problem but a great way to relax. It was our home life, with Garry's fast-paced work schedule, that was stressful.

CHAPTER NINETEEN

OUR FAMILY HAD OUTGROWN our home on Arcola Avenue, and I thought having more space would help Garry relax. I wanted to stay in the neighborhood, and when I found a house on Sarah Street, next door to where my friend Jackie Joseph and her husband, actor Ken Berry, lived, I asked if I could peek over their fence. Jackie said, "You know, my house is going to be for sale soon, too, because Ken and I are getting divorced."

I was sad for their marriage but fell in love with their house, where I still live today. It was on an acre of land, with a swimming pool and enough room to build a tennis court. The house had an English country feeling to it and, while spacious, didn't feel too large. Jackie told me the home had once been owned by Disney Studios and that Julie Andrews had lived there while filming *Mary Poppins*. I thought that was a good omen.

My husband was working very long hours, so I had to find more and more things to keep myself busy. I began to do charity work in the community on issues related to children and healthcare and volunteered for more jobs at Kathleen and Scott's school, Oakwood, a private school with classes from kindergarten through 12th grade. All three of our kids went to elementary school there.

I was on the board and had spent many years fundraising for Oakwood, but when it came time to send Lori to junior high and high school, I wanted to find a well-established school that wouldn't need any major fundraising campaigns. The day Garry and I toured the Westlake School for Girls, near Beverly Hills, I knew I had found a great fit. The academic curriculum was topnotch, and the campus was beautiful.

"Garry, this is perfect. And look at these buildings. I won't have to do any fundraising," I said.

We sent in Lori's application and were thrilled when she was accepted. A month or so before she was due to start seventh grade, the administration tore half the school down and announced a capital campaign to rebuild. We had paid thousands of dollars for her to go to classes in trailers. I couldn't believe it.

"What do you think happened?" I asked Garry.

"They saw you coming," he said. "'Oh, look at the nice rich lady. Let's put her in charge of fundraising.'" We laughed but could not get over the fact that all the private schools in Los Angeles seemed focused on raising money.

I eventually joined the Westlake board, too. I was a bit more comfortable with wealthy people than Garry. It was typical for me to be one of the only women on the board, but I felt it was easy to communicate with these men who worked in the industry with Garry. I understood their work pressures and their home life, and I could be empathetic and a good listener. The meetings were a good way to remain stimulated mentally while still busy raising my children.

I did renew my nursing license every year, on the chance I might find myself wanting to return to my career. I didn't know how or when, but I didn't want to let my license lapse.

At one point, when he had four shows on the air, Garry literally employed hundreds of people. Despite all his power and wealth, he remained a very down-to-earth person, who truly cared about his employees. His favorite day of the week was Saturday, when his friends and co-workers would come to our house and play basketball on the half-court he had built in our backyard. He was still a little boy at heart, who loved to play sports despite his fragile health.

As for his health, we still struggled with one thing during the 1980s, and that was Garry's smoking. At one time, we had both been smokers. But I started smoking because the nursing students who smoked got more breaks; I never loved smoking like Garry did. When I started having kids, I just stopped. It wasn't even because we knew it was bad for pregnant women back then. I simply didn't like the taste of cigarettes while I was pregnant. I stopped buying cigarettes for me but continued buying them for Garry.

With Scott, Lori, and Kathleen. This picture was taken on Sarah Street, in the front yard of our new home, which we bought from actors Jackie Joseph and Ken Berry.

All three of our children went to Oakwood for elementary school. This picture was taken in 1981 at Scott's sixth-grade graduation.

Actually, when the kids were little, I started smoking again, very briefly. Having Kathleen and Scott just a year apart took a toll on my body, and my doctor said a hysterectomy was inevitable. I had always suffered from endometriosis, and it was getting worse, and a hysterectomy would resolve the problem.

With three little kids at home, the hospital stay felt like a vacation. I had a girlfriend bring me some Hershey bars with almonds, potato chips, a six-pack of Coke, and two packs of Salem Menthol, my favorite. You could still smoke in a hospital room then, and I had a huge room, where I entertained visitors. I had not had a cigarette in six years, but I started smoking again right there in the hospital, and those cigarettes tasted terrific.

I remember my time in the hospital so clearly. My next-door neighbor Margo Kurtz came to visit me after the surgery. She was a lovely woman, whose daughter, Swoosie Kurtz, was starting to get some work in the theater, and it was exciting for Margo and her husband, Frank, to see their daughter's career blossoming. Margo sat at the end of my bed, and we watched Trisha Nixon's wedding on the television. While my children were home with Garry, I sat in the hospital with Margo, smoking, eating, watching TV, and having a great time. My children didn't even know I ever smoked. And once I was discharged from the hospital, I never smoked again. But Garry was another story.

Garry tried to quit smoking several times. The first program he tried was with a company called Schick. When he failed with that, he moved on to a program called QuitNow, and later to a program called Smokenders. None of them could help him stop smoking, but all invited him to come back and try again, free of charge, because he was so entertaining and such a good sport. He was so competitive that he was always the best student in the program; he tried hardest and never missed a meeting. The only problem was that he would start smoking again the minute the program ended. He tried individual therapy and group therapy, but nothing could keep him from lighting up.

The children tried to be helpful. When Post-it notes came out, Lori would stick little notes that read "Daddy, please stop smoking" all over his desk. And we were all very supportive of the different methods each program used. One time, a company suggested he bury his cigarettes in the backyard. We thought this was a terrific idea until we looked out the window one night to see Garry using a shovel, because he was so desperate for a smoke.

Eventually, he met a woman named Carol Williard. She would come to his office each day for an hour, during which he could take no phone calls. They would talk about life and their families, and how Carol was able to stop smoking and learned to help others do it, too. She instructed him to carry a pack of cigarettes in the breast pocket of his blazer. If someone asked him for a cigarette, he was to give them one. But he was making a choice not to smoke one himself. For months, he carried a pack of stale cigarettes in his jacket pocket.

Then they decided Garry would carry toothpicks in his pocket as a replacement for his cigarettes. He began to collect toothpick holders, carrying a different one in his pocket each day. Carol went on to help Henry Winkler stop smoking, too. It was almost a miracle that this one special woman became the only person in the world who could help Garry quit smoking. When she got married and Garry walked her down the aisle, it seemed the perfect moment to celebrate how much she had done for Garry's life.

He stopped smoking when he was 50, in 1984. It probably helped that *Laverne & Shirley*'s eight-season run had ended the year before, as had the two seasons of *Joanie Loves Chachi*, and *Mork & Mindy*'s last episode was in 1982. (*Happy Days* concluded its run that September.) Garry and I were in Venice, Italy, staying at a hotel along the Grand Canal, when Carol called from California to see how we were doing. She asked if Garry wanted a cigarette, and he said he was fine without one. It was wonderful.

Even though he was young for it, people started giving Garry life-achievement awards and honoring him at benefits as he entered his late forties. It was an advantage to have Garry at an event, because he could fill tables at any gala with the casts from his television shows.

In 1982, Garry's friend Phil Foster, who played Penny's dad on Laverne & Shirley, wanted Garry to be honored by the Los Angeles Free Clinic. A friend I knew from another charity group was involved with the clinic as well, so I asked her to give me a tour. I wanted to see what the Free Clinic was all about before Garry agreed.

My friend took me to see the Free Clinic's High Risk Youth Program, which served many teenagers and children living on the streets of Los Angeles. I met two social workers, Laurie and Susan, and a doctor named Eric, and I could tell that all three thought I was just a fancy Hollywood do-gooder who didn't want to get her hands dirty. But I felt an instant connection to the clinic and its mission. For the first time since I had left Cedars, I felt excited at the potential for a new job in medicine. I called the following week and asked if the clinic could use a volunteer nurse. When the answer was yes, I started the next day.

By this time, Lori had gone off to Chicago and college at Northwestern, and Kathleen and Scott were in junior high, so I had time on my hands. The Free Clinic was open twice a week, but I started working just one day. But when I heard the staff discussing interesting patients on Thursdays, I volunteered for that day, too. Sometimes, after work, the staff went out to dinner or celebrated a birthday together. They were all younger than I was, and it felt exhilarating to be with a group of professionals who had so much energy and were so dedicated to their careers and to giving homeless children medical care.

I felt I finally had something all my own, independent of Garry and my children. The job came along at a perfect time in my life, when Kathleen and Scott were learning to drive and more focused on their sports, friends, and college applications than on staying home with me.

I wore my old nursing-school pin on my lab coat. It had been sitting in my jewelry box for years, and I thought it was time that I brought it out of the dark. It made me feel grateful for all I had now.

Standing proud with the social workers and doctors I worked with at the Los Angeles Free Clinic. From left: Laurie Goodman, Dr. Richard MacKenzie, Gary Yates, me, Susan Pearlman, and Dr. Eric Cohen.

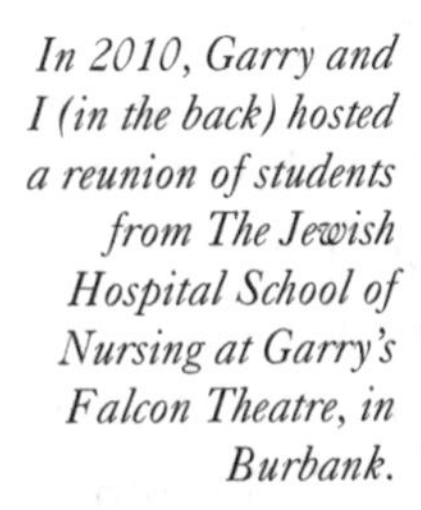

In 2010, Garry and I (in the back) hosted a reunion of students from The Jewish Hospital School of Nursing at Garry's Falcon Theatre, in Burbank.

Several of us got together for a Jewish Hospital student-nurse reunion in 2007.

Back when I was a young nursing student at The Jewish Hospital, I never would have dreamed that one day I would be married to a Hollywood director, have three nearly grown children, and work alongside dedicated people like those I met at the L.A. Free Clinic. I couldn't help thinking that all the good things in my life had occurred because I had decided to become a nurse.

The pin reminded me of all this. However, the pin would not be around for long. One day, I went to the car wash, and the next time I put on my lab coat, the pin was gone. I had hung onto it for nearly 20 years and managed to lose it in a single afternoon. I wondered if it was a sign that I should contact my old school. When I called to order a new pin, it opened the door to something else entirely.

I still received the alumni newsletter, edited by a group of women I kept in touch with. And I had corresponded with the director of nurses, Helen Rigdon, ever since I graduated. It was through my friendship with Helen that I came up with an idea. I had been given a scholarship for my second and third years at The Jewish Hospital, and maybe I could do the same for another nursing student.

Several years earlier, Garry and I had set up a family foundation through which we had made donations to his alma mater, Northwestern University; to the Los Angeles Music Center; and to our children's schools, the Westlake School for Girls and the Oakwood School. We had never given any money to my nursing school. Just the idea of this tickled me, because I had been so broke as a student that I nearly didn't get to go to school at all. The idea that I could in some way give back to the school that had changed my life seemed exactly the right thing to do.

Over the next several years, my $10,000 donation paid for several scholarships, until, unfortunately, the school had to close its doors because enrollment was too low. When I heard about it, I contacted some of my old nursing friends. It was clear there was nothing we could do to keep the school open; instead, we organized a weekend party to celebrate all the years our school had been turning students into nurses.

Of the 48 graduates in my year, almost 20 nurses came back that weekend. Some of the women I had kept in touch with, but others I hadn't seen since we'd waved goodbye in 1961. At the big dinner on Saturday night, many of us gave speeches sharing stories about our nursing-school days. I described how I had gotten the $100 to pay for my first year's tuition by working at Camp Sunshine.

Throughout the weekend, there were many tears but also much laughter as we remembered doing things like injecting oranges. On Sunday afternoon, we had a tour. Later that day, we had a tea and an auction to sell off the school's furniture, items such as silver tea services, and other mementos. Most pieces were priced low to move; I think the most expensive item was a big punchbowl that went for $500.

When Garry and I had made our donation, scholarships were $1,000 a year. I was a little nervous wondering where the remainder of our money might go, and Helen said she would investigate. Much to our surprise, she told us that our money had been invested and had grown to more than $100,000. I said, "I wish they could invest all my money with that rate of return."

The school decided to use some of the money to build bookcases to display memorabilia from the nursing school in the new hospital. The rest was put into a fund to pay for an annual nursing conference in my name, the Barbara Marshall Seminar, dedicated to education on new topics in nursing care. Over the years, I have attended several of the seminars and always found it wonderful to connect with others at the event. I will always have so many happy memories from my time in nursing school.

Sometimes I wonder if I hadn't had the opportunity to become a nurse, what would I have become? I could have joined the Peace Corps, or become a social worker, but I don't think anything would have been as rewarding as nursing. The truth is that I fell into nursing, because I couldn't afford to go to college and become a teacher. It proved to be a very lucky fall. When I look back at some of my high school friends who never left Cincinnati, I get a real glimpse of what my life would have been like without nursing in it.

When I took my final tour of the student dorms before they closed the nursing school, I made a point of going to the room I had shared with Maureen. Most of the rooms still had the furniture we had used, and when I saw mine, I remembered how I'd thought it was the greatest room in the world. Never before had I had my own bed, my own dresser and four drawers, my own desk, and especially my own bookshelf.

At the auction later that day, I purchased 14 of the bookshelves to give to my nursing friends. I kept one for myself, and it sits in the entryway of my home. When I pass it, at least once a day, it reminds me that even though I'm not wearing white or working in a hospital anymore, I'm so very proud to call myself a nurse.

CHAPTER TWENTY

ONE DAY, GARRY CAME home and told us that he was done with television. This came as no surprise, because we could see his television shows were winding down, and Garry often talked about retirement. The problem was that he didn't like to play golf and being on a sailboat made him seasick. We couldn't imagine what he would do if he retired. That day, he announced his plan: He was going to become a movie director. At the age of 47, he was given his first movie to direct. It was called *Young Doctors in Love*.

I looked at him and said, "Do you think you know how to direct a movie?"

He said, "Not exactly. But I'm going to give it a shot."

As Garry was starting to talk about directing a movie, we were feeling the effects of his television success. We had money, lots of money. However, money was not something either of us had much experience with or knew much about. I grew up barely scraping by, and while his family was middle class, they never really knew what it was like to have plenty of money in the bank. His father always had schemes that didn't pan out. They had a big house once and lost it. After Garry's success with his television shows, we had an abundance of money for the first time in either of our lives.

When I look back on that time, I see how inexperienced we were in financial matters. Not long after buying the house on Arcola Avenue, we did what many people in Hollywood do: We hired a business manager to oversee and invest our money. We asked around, interviewed some firms, and chose Richard "Dick" Cohen of the firm Cohen & Baizer, in Beverly Hills. Eventually, we grew closer to his partner, Neil Baizer. Over time, Neil became a close family friend as well.

Neil was a confident, smooth-talking man who told us to "sit back and relax." His self-assurance was like Jeremy Piven's in *Entourage*.

He made you feel he knew what was best, and in the beginning, honestly, Garry was earning so much, it was a relief not to have to worry about what to do with it. We trusted Neil with our money and never doubted his skill for a moment.

One of the first extravagant things we bought was a second home, a townhouse on the beach in Malibu near Moonshadows restaurant. Garry and I liked staying in small hotels in Malibu, but the more often we went, the more Malibu felt like our special place. Garry's close friend Jack Klugman had lived near the Malibu pier for years, and Garry often spent afternoons with Jack in his condo. Buying a beach house made so much sense to us. Neil helped us structure the purchase and encouraged it, viewing it as a sound investment.

The townhouse needed some decorating, so I brought in Lil Chain, the interior decorator who had done my homes in Toluca Lake. Just the thought of using a decorator again made Garry break out in a rash, but I convinced him the beach house needed sprucing up, which it did.

Lil did a great job with the place, making it feel warm, with large prints of flowers and birds and comfortable green sofas. We began going there on weekends and holidays. Scott started surfing, and we even bought a jet ski. Garry was never much for water sports, but he enjoyed walking on the beach and feeling the sun on his face. His olive Italian skin tanned well, while I kept my white midwestern skin covered with clothing and sunscreen.

A few years earlier, in the mid-1970s, we had started taking the kids to the Kahala Hilton, a resort on the Hawaiian island of Oahu, each Christmas. It became a wonderful, albeit very expensive, holiday pilgrimage for us. Our beach house became a way to extend the relaxation we felt during our Christmases in Hawaii.

In Malibu one weekend, Garry bumped into his old friend Debbie Reynolds, and she invited us to dinner at her house, just up the beach from Jack's condo. This was the house in which she had raised her children, Carrie and Todd, after her divorce from Eddie Fisher, who left her to marry Elizabeth Taylor. The house was lovely, right on Carbon Beach along Pacific Coast Highway. My tastes never ran very modern, and what I loved most about it was that it felt like it was on Cape Cod. It had wood-beamed ceilings and a brown thatched roof, with a swimming pool, four bedrooms, and an office.

And it had a lot of character. Debbie was very petite, so all the light switches had been installed lower than normal. One bathroom was entirely padded with antique patchwork quilts. There were also signs of the children. A crawl space that led to the attic had a warning written in block letters: "Carrie's hide out. No adults aloud."

Debbie gave us a tour and then announced that she was putting the house on the market; it was too big to live in alone. We had owned our townhouse for more than a year, and the time felt right to consider buying a bigger place. Although Debbie's house was expensive, selling the townhouse would help with the down payment. It just felt like the right house for us at the time, and surely a smart investment. Neil agreed and helped us structure the deal to buy it.

Garry was very excited but was often embarrassed by the size and location of the house. A side of him wanted to be rich and famous in Hollywood, but another side remained a little sick kid from the Bronx. With his mixed feelings about wealth, Garry often told people that we shared the house with two other families. In his mind, it was over the top somehow to be able to afford such a large second home.

The children thought it was funny when he fibbed about owning the house, pretending we were not as rich as we were. Nevertheless, we did own that house, and Garry loved it. He said he would talk to the waves and look for solutions to work problems when he was at the beach. It was a very special place for him to relax, reflect, and recharge. We spent time there on our own, with the children and, later, their spouses, and eventually with our six grandchildren, who adored the house.

Garry often told a funny story about using his new wealth to buy his parents something. He approached his father first.

"Pop, I have some extra money, and I would like to buy you something special. What can I buy you? What is your dream?"

"A white Cadillac," said Tony without a second's hesitation.

Then Garry went to his mother and made her the same offer.

"Ma, I have some extra money, and I want to buy you something special. What is your dream? Dad asked for a white Cadillac."

His mother paused and considered the thoughtful gesture of her oldest child. "My dream is that I don't want your father to get the white Cadillac," Marjorie said.

That story epitomizes the relationship between Garry's parents. They never liked each other very much, but they were certainly proud of their son's success and loved receiving gifts from him. The fact that he was able to get both his sisters work on his television shows made Garry's parents so proud.

Like Garry's parents, my parents had something of a rollercoaster relationship. In the later years of his life, my dad worked as a loading-dock manager for a trucking company. When he retired from that job, he literally had nothing to do. Since he had never learned to drive, he couldn't go anywhere on his own. One day, we found out his buddies were picking him up and taking him to the racetrack, where they drank beer all day long.

Once, my mom called from Cincinnati in the middle of the night and woke me up.

"Your dad is lying on the ground outside the house," she announced, "just laughing and giggling. He pulled the gutter off the roof, and I can't get him to come inside."

"Mom, I'm in California. I can't do anything to help you right now. You need to go outside and get him into the house," I said.

Calls like this continued, and it really began to worry me. I was rather shocked by my dad's drinking, because growing up, I never saw him drink at all. I called my sister Brenda, and we agreed that he needed to learn how to drive to become more independent. I bought him a Pinto, and Brenda taught him to drive it.

However, this new independence led to more trouble: He started driving himself to the racetrack and coming home drunk. One day, my mom saw him driving home from the track with their five-year-

In 2000, I made a visit to the farm and reunited with my dad, my brother Stephen, my sisters, Gloria and Brenda, and my mom. Gloria was (and still is) a big Barry Manilow fan, as you can see from her T-shirt.

Garry and I often took the children to Kentucky to visit my parents on the farm.

old grandchild in the car, and that put an end to his driving.

Garry offered some advice. "Why don't you ask your dad what he would like to do?"

I posed the question to my dad, and he replied, "I think I would like to move to Kentucky. I have a few nephews and other relatives there."

"But what would you do there? Other than visiting relatives," I asked.

"Maybe if I had a small farm with just a few chickens and a cow—that would keep me busy," he said.

I consulted Garry, and he said it would be fine, though he cautioned me, "Just don't buy the first place you see."

That is exactly what I did. I met my sisters in Kentucky, and the first place we found, in Richmond, was perfect. It was a wonderful property, on about 100 acres with a farm, two barns, and a new house. Neil said he thought the farm was a good investment, and he flew to Kentucky with me to see it and visit my family. Later, I moved my dad from Cincinnati down to the farm.

This plan worked for a while, until my mother noticed how often Garry and the children and I were going to the farm. Mom was jealous of all the attention Dad was getting from us, so she moved to the farm, too. It was not an ideal situation, but my father, always a soft-spoken man who never asked for anything, handled my mother the best he could. Mom would go up to Cincinnati on Wednesdays and get her hair done and go bowling with her girlfriends, then drive back to the farm on Thursday mornings. Dad's most peaceful day was Wednesday, when she was out of the state.

When Garry and I were first married, we used to dream about what we would buy if we ever had any money. I used to say a mink coat, because in the 1960s it was very fashionable to have one. On our tenth wedding anniversary, he bought me a mink coat. He loved surprising me with gifts and having the kids in on it. Later, he bought me a sable coat from a fancier furrier in New York City. He loved giving me diamond and gold pieces from Tiffany for Christmas,

We threw my dad a party in Kentucky for his 80th birthday. My mother, never camera shy, pushed my dad to the back row so she could be front and center.

Valentine's Day, and my birthday. When I was a little girl growing up in Ohio, I never saw a Tiffany box, let alone silver or gold jewelry from the store. When I understood what the name Tiffany meant, it felt special whenever Garry brought home a little turquoise bag.

While Garry loved surprising me, from time to time I wanted to surprise him, too. He often went to premieres and other red-carpet events, and his office would rent a limo. One year, we decided to surprise Garry with his own limousine. I can still see Neil and his son driving it through the gates of our house on Christmas morning. It felt like a big deal that Garry was big enough to have his own limo. It was dark blue, and a few years later, we bought him a silver one. We hired different drivers, and when it wasn't being used, it sat in our driveway—a symbol that we were now officially Hollywood players.

Then the studios started giving Garry expensive gifts. Michael Eisner had left Paramount for The Walt Disney Company, where he was chairman and CEO, and one day in the mid- or late '80s, Garry said that Michael had offered to buy him a car. When I asked Garry what kind he'd asked for, he said, "A Volkswagen."

"A Volkswagen?! Are you kidding me? Why did you say that?"

"It's the only name of a car I could think of," he said.

"Well, you call Eisner back right now and tell him you want a Mercedes."

"Really?"

"Yes. And make it powder blue."

"Are you sure? That sounds expensive," he said.

"Yes. I'm sure," I said.

Garry called Eisner, and a few days later, a light blue Mercedes was in our driveway.

Our life changed in other tangible ways. We started to fly first class. Sometimes the studio bought the tickets, but other times we paid for the tickets ourselves.

The children continued going to private schools. While Scott stayed on at Oakwood for high school, Kathleen followed Lori into the Westlake School for Girls. When they were old enough, each got a car, so they could drive themselves over the hill to school. The tuitions were expensive, and the obligation to contribute to each school's annual giving and capital campaigns was constant and persistent. And we were now entering different social circles. The other parents weren't only other writers and television producers; they were famous actors, well-known directors, and the heads of studios and other major corporations.

The number of people on our payroll grew. I still had a full-time, live-in housekeeper and a full-time gardener, and by the early 1980s, a large staff of secretaries and punch-up writers was working with Garry in his new office, nearby on Riverside Drive. (His staff would grow whenever he directed a movie, then diminish again when he finished filming and began the editing process.)

Marjorie had been showing signs of Alzheimer's disease since the late '70s. She'd seemed mystified by the success of *Laverne & Shirley*; I remember her making zany comments like "I don't know why they let Penny do this show. She's a jailbird." When she was diagnosed with Alzheimer's, that made more sense, although of course it added a whole new layer of stress for Garry. He thought his mother had an intuitively sharp mind, and seeing it disintegrate was painful for all of us.

We moved her into an assisted-living facility, and one of Garry's secretaries moved in to watch over her. Before that, we never knew when we would get a strange phone call—someone saying, "She's on Ventura Boulevard hanging onto a telephone pole and screaming, 'Help me! Help me!'" When her disease required professional help, we were very grateful we had the money to support her with full-time care at home.

A few years later, when Garry's father had a stroke, we hired round-the-clock caregivers to live with him in his house. Even before his stroke, Tony had made Garry promise he would do everything he could to allow Tony to live out his days in his own home, in Toluca Lake. With help from Ronny and Penny, Garry did just that. Tony was never a very nice man, and he often acted like a big shot in a way that Garry, despite his success, never did. But Garry considered loyalty to family among the most important obligations anyone could have. He took care of Tony until the end of his life and in the way he had asked for.

In November 1983, Garry was honored with a star along Hollywood Boulevard's Walk of Fame.

CHAPTER TWENTY-ONE

MEANWHILE, GARRY WAS WORKING on *Young Doctors in Love*, which spoofed hospital soap operas. It starred Michael McKean, who had played Lenny in *Laverne & Shirley*, and Sean Young. Garry cast dozens of his friends in cameo roles. Hector Elizondo appeared in all 18 of the movies Garry directed.

Garry wanted me and our children to appear in the movie as well. I have to say, it was not the best experience for any of us. First of all, most of the movie was filmed in Downey, which is only 25 or 30 miles south of Toluca Lake but very difficult to get to. Garry started coming home at 3 a.m. and wondered why I didn't have dinner on the table.

We were completely out of sync. Kathleen and Scott never saw him. On the weekends, he wanted to know who those people were playing so loudly in the front yard while he was trying to sleep. I said, "Those are your children." Garry would kick the dog, yell at the kids, smoke cigarettes, and eat ice cream. We eventually found out the ice cream was making him sick, because he was lactose intolerant. But that didn't solve the other problems.

Young Doctors in Love was one of the first movies Jerry Bruckheimer produced. He and Garry were like two freshmen in a big high school, trying to figure out where to go and what to do without any guidance. One day, Garry called a director friend, Francis Ford Coppola, and asked his advice. Francis said, "You are going to be on your feet a lot, so change your shoes." And that was good advice, but only the tip of the iceberg as far as what Garry had to learn about directing a movie. We had grown accustomed to the routine and pace of his television schedule, but directing a movie was all-encompassing. I wasn't sure I ever wanted him to do another one.

When filming concluded, we stayed to see the gag reel, or outtakes, at the cast party, and then we went to our beach house, just the two of us. Because of his allergies, Garry had not been able to eat anything at the party, so I made him scrambled eggs and bacon, and while he was eating, I shared my concerns with him.

"This is the last time you're going to direct a movie," I said. "I can't live like this. You can't live like this. I think you should go back to television."

"There's no going back to television," he said. "I've done everything I wanted to do in television. Directing is hard on us, I understand. But I think I can do better on the next one."

"What next one?"

"I have another script," he said. "It's called *The Flamingo Kid*."

"Well, then, this time I think you should stay in a hotel. Where you can order room service and they can take care of you," I said.

"I will be staying in a hotel. It shoots in New York."

"New York?! How are you going to do that?"

"I'm not sure. But I will figure it out as I go," he said.

Filming *The Flamingo Kid*, starring Matt Dillon and Richard Crenna, was like night and day compared to when Garry was making *Young Doctors in Love*. Diane Perkins, Garry's longtime secretary and assistant, moved to New York with him and they stayed at the Parker Meridien Hotel, in midtown. Garry loved being in New York City and was able to keep a healthier and more stable schedule as they shot scenes there and in Far Rockaway, Long Island. I could maintain my life in Los Angeles, while, because they were shooting in the summertime, the kids and I had more flexibility for visiting him. My visits were met with excitement, and Garry and I enjoyed catching up after the weeks apart. It made me think he should always direct his films out of town.

And something magical happened, too: He was able to figure out how to tell a wonderful story as a director, on a film he hadn't written, and make a movie even some critics applauded and appreciated. The positive feedback made him realize he wanted to keep directing movies. From then on, to show how much he appreciated my support, he dedicated each of his films to me in the closing credits.

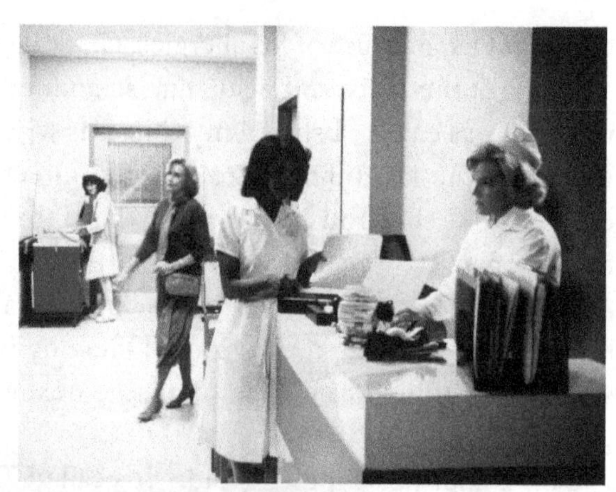

My first acting job for Garry was in his third film, Nothing in Common, *in 1986. I wore my own cap. That's Eva Marie Saint approaching the nurses' desk.*

In 1987, I drove to Mendocino to visit Garry on the set of Overboard. *Here we're with Scott and the film's stars, Goldie Hawn and Kurt Russell.*

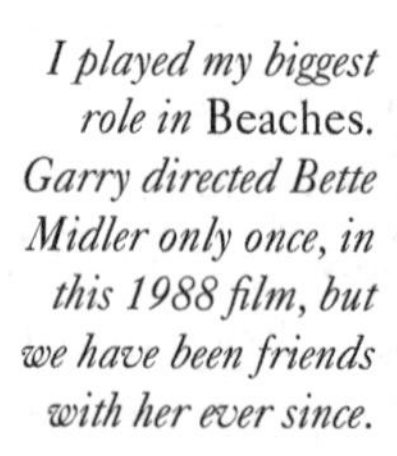

I played my biggest role in Beaches. *Garry directed Bette Midler only once, in this 1988 film, but we have been friends with her ever since.*

In 2004, Julie Andrews and I sported several fancy hats on the set of Princess Diaries 2.

In 2009, I played a nurse again in Valentine's Day. *The all-star cast included Jennifer Garner.*

I appeared with Oscar winners Hilary Swank (left) and Halle Berry in Garry's 2011 holiday romance New Year's Eve.

He always used my maiden name, Barbara Sue Wells. He liked doing that, he said, because my friends from nursing school could see I was part of his movie career.

Around this time, something peculiar occurred. It was such a small thing that at first it almost didn't make me pause. While Lori was away at college, I had hired her boyfriend, Doug, to help with some tasks. Doug went on to become a very successful businessman, but at the time, he was just doing errands for me.

One afternoon, he came back and said, "The strangest thing happens when I go to the bank for you."

"What do you mean?" I asked.

"It takes so long for them to cash your checks. Whether the check is for $20 or $2,000, the teller always goes to the bank manager."

"But they always cash the check," I confirmed.

"Yes. But it takes a long time. I think something is wrong," he said.

Something was indeed very wrong, but it took me awhile to figure out what the problem was. I had a feeling even then, though, that it had to do with a real estate deal in Pasadena, something Neil had mentioned to me once in referring to buying a building. But I kept my concerns to myself, because Garry was starting to shoot another film, in Chicago.

Nothing in Common starred an up-and-coming actor named Tom Hanks. Garry knew him well from the lot at Paramount Studios, where Tom had made his early-'80s television show, *Bosom Buddies*. After Garry hired him for the lead, we went out to dinner with Tom and his wife, Samantha, in Chicago. I had been married to Garry long enough that I had grown quite comfortable going to dinner with actors and their spouses. We had a lovely dinner; however, throughout the meal I was getting a strange vibe from the two. I can be a little clairvoyant sometimes, and I just had to share my feelings with Garry.

"So what did you think?" Garry asked as we walked back to the hotel.

"They were very nice. But I want to warn you about something,"

I said.

"What?"

"They are going to get divorced, so prepare yourself. Tom is not going to be in the best mood while he is making this movie."

And sure enough, I was right. Tom and Samantha divorced, and he married Rita Wilson the following year. I think from that moment on, Garry began to trust my psychic powers. He began consulting me on casting, as well as on actors and actresses who were not getting along on a set.

Getting Tom to star in the film was the easy part. The hard part was getting Jackie Gleason to play Tom's father. He said he was too tired and too sick and had no interest in being in the film. Garry flew to Florida to meet with him and brought the script. Again, Jackie said he wasn't interested.

"Jackie, look, I get it. You're a great man. And now you're tired and you're sick and you don't want to make another movie," Garry told him. "But this is a terrific role for you. If you don't do this movie, your obituary will say that your last movie was *Smokey and the Bandit II*. Is that what you want to be remembered for?"

Jackie paused for a moment and then agreed to do the movie. Once Garry convinced him to sign on, they were all set. Adding Eva Marie Saint, Bess Armstrong, and Sela Ward made the cast even stronger.

The Flamingo Kid had given Garry more confidence in his skills directing a movie. He realized he did have what it takes, even when some of the crew disagreed with him. *Nothing in Common* gave the industry confidence in his ability to direct a major motion picture with big movie stars.

Meanwhile, Garry and I had made a financial commitment to the building campaign for the Westlake School for Girls, and after one of the board meetings, the headmaster, Nate Reynolds, asked to speak with me.

"Barbara," he said, "I'm having a bit of a problem. Your pledge money never came through. When I called your business manager to ask about it, he said I would have to wait until January."

"That's odd," I said. "He should have sent it to you already."

"Neil said I shouldn't tell you about it. But I felt I had to."

"Thank you, Nate. I'm glad you did. I'll look into it immediately."

I thought about what Nate had just told me. January was the time of year the big checks from Garry's television shows came in.

When Garry came home from Chicago for Christmas, I had to say something about Doug's difficulties at the bank and the delayed check to Westlake. When you put the two together, it pointed to a larger problem. I just didn't know the extent of the problem.

When I told Garry, he threw a script across the room. "What are you talking about?!" he said angrily.

"I think Neil has done something with our money," I said.

"You are supposed to be watching things. Figure it out!"

Garry was so tired and working so hard that he didn't even have the mental capability to have a conversation about our finances. It was not as if Neil was a stranger who just started doing crazy things with our money. He was our most trusted financial advisor and our close friend; he visited Garry on the sets of his movies and met privately with his theatrical lawyers and agents. I knew if I was going to go up against Neil, I couldn't do it on my own.

The next morning, I asked Garry to call his childhood friend Martin Garbus, an eminent lawyer. (In fact, he was considered one of the best criminal- and constitutional-law attorneys in the country.) Garry explained that he didn't know what was going on, but that we needed Marty's help. We were very fortunate that a boy who had grown up with Garry in the Bronx had turned into such an impressive lawyer.

It was while Garry was making *Nothing in Common* that our money troubles became overwhelming. I had to hide them, because he needed to focus on his film. I ended up not talking to him much during that period as I worked with Marty to try to unravel what was going on.

Marty and I met with Dick and Neil in their office, letting them know we thought there were problems. Then we went to the bank and found out that Garry and I had been living on an open-ended line of credit. As it turns out, we were not only broke, we were millions of dollars in debt.

CHAPTER TWENTY-TWO

MY WORK AT THE Free Clinic was my refuge during 1986 and 1987. Sometimes when my friends Susan and Laurie asked how I was, I would burst into tears. As hard as that time was, working helped take my mind off my own troubles. Talking with young men and women who lived on the streets and improving their access to medical care felt important to me, and significant. Also, some of my co-workers didn't know that I had legal and financial troubles. They just saw me as a nurse, and I clung to that identity.

Garry was never ashamed, in the way a banker or lawyer or someone else might be, about a failed business deal. During the five years it took to untangle our involvement in the real estate project and fight our legal and financial battles, he was not shy telling people about our problems.

Garry knew that business and finance were not his forte. He was a creative person who placed a high value on his skills as a writer, a director, and even an actor. He was excited when Albert Brooks asked him to appear in his 1985 film *Lost in America*. The role as the casino owner was small, but Garry made it memorable. In the film, when Albert and his wife lose all their money at the casino, Albert goes to Garry to ask for it back. Garry says sternly, "Who do you think I am? *Santie* Claus?"

Garry found acting in other people's movies relaxing. He enjoyed being on another director's set and seeing everything from the actor's point of view. Now he started taking acting jobs to make some quick money, too.

When Garry was home between movies, he would grow very angry with me about the money problems. I decided it was best to keep him working—not only to keep money coming in but as a way to distract him. After *Nothing in Common*, he signed on to direct *Overboard*, a comedy with Goldie Hawn and Kurt Russell. Most of the filming took place in Mendocino, a seaside town in Northern California. It was on that movie that we decided, whether he was filming on location or in Los Angeles, Garry would stay in a hotel. When he was filming in L.A., his home away from home became the Sheraton Universal Hotel, a five-minute drive from our house. I would do his laundry when he came home on weekends. During the week, he could get 24-hour room service, and nobody cared what time he got in at night or left in the morning. And we could easily visit him, sometimes even for dinner if the shooting wrapped early that day.

We had to tell the children about our money troubles, because they were old enough to know and there was really no use in hiding it. We said we would continue to live our lives as we were, if on a much smaller scale. We would live on the line of credit, but we sold the limousine and started cutting back on purchases. We still went to Hawaii for Christmas, but we didn't stay as long. Garry tried to demonstrate that we didn't have to give one another big gifts by buying frames and photo cubes and filling them with photographs of our family. These were among the children's favorite holiday presents from Garry, and they still treasure them.

Garry was also a very big letter writer. He wrote us letters and notes for special occasions and throughout the year. If there was a birthday or a holiday, he would write a special poem for the celebrant or just for the day. His poems were not fancy or traditional but rather clunky, funny, and true. He would write them on note cards or, more often, on lined notebook paper, sometimes even on napkins. Garry's words were important and powerful, and anything he could do to express his love and loyalty came through with his pen. He loved not only the look of his signature but also his personalized stationery and notepaper.

By now, Lori was in graduate school at Northwestern, Kathleen was an undergraduate there, and Scott soon joined them. In addition to protecting Garry from our money problems so that he could concentrate on his films, I protected the children so they could concentrate on their schoolwork. When I wasn't at the Free Clinic, I spent most of my waking hours going to meetings with Marty. I knew I was mentally strong enough to handle the pressure, and that armed with Marty's legal expertise, we had a chance of putting our lives back together.

My intuition about the investment in Pasadena had been right: The city was revitalizing part of its Old Town, and every time a check came in from one of Garry's movies or television shows, Neil would put the money into the development project. Funded by our money, the developers went to Europe and bought buildings full of furniture, even antique elevators.

What probably began as a legitimate investment opportunity turned into a nightmare for us when Neil crossed the line. We had no idea about what was going on, and to make matters worse, his actions were not technically illegal. During a vacation in Italy, we had given him our power of attorney, and he had never rescinded it.

I think Neil didn't report any problems to us early on because he thought he was investing our money well. Now I was faced with figuring out exactly was what going on. Marty set up a meeting in Pasadena with some of our real estate partners, none of whom I had ever met. As soon as we walked into the room, where about six men were sitting at a table, one of them threw a folder across the table toward me and said, "You owe me one million dollars!" I was taken aback, especially because the man and I had never laid eyes on each other.

I thought how far I had come from my roots, a man I had never met accusing me of owing him a million dollars. Marty gently took my arm and led me out of the meeting, our first and last one. Strategically, he knew what to do every step of the way.

Marty had already gone to Garry's theatrical agents and stopped the checks from going directly to Cohen & Baizer. He and other lawyers talked to us about the possibility of declaring personal bankruptcy. I had terrible nightmares about that, about what would happen if we did file for bankruptcy. I just couldn't imagine throwing in the towel like that. Privately, Garry met with many friends and acquaintances to see if anyone would be interested in buying the buildings we owned in Pasadena.

One night, I dreamed that a short, dark man came through the back door of Garry's suite of offices and said he was willing to take them off our hands. I prayed quietly that the short, dark man would show up soon, because if we could not sell the buildings, we were faced with only one outcome: personal bankruptcy.

Garry and I tried to compartmentalize our emotions and focus on the positive: We had our children. We had our health. We had our house. He was working, and he would keep working. Those were the important things to remember.

During the endless legal battles, Garry and I definitely had arguments at home. During the worst fight, he told me that I should get my own lawyer, but he just said it in the heat of the moment. I knew he didn't mean it. I'm an optimist, and I had confidence in our lawyer and his ability to navigate us through this crisis. Garry was always a worrier, and I knew I had to work hard to protect him from being overwhelmed by it.

And then, just like in my dream, a short, dark man arrived to save the day. His name was Doug Stitzel, and he was a real estate developer. He came in the back door of Garry's offices on Riverside Drive and explained that he had been the developer of Two Rodeo, a collection of high-end stores in an outdoor shopping center in Beverly Hills. Now he wanted to move to his next project. He said, "I heard you are trying to get rid of some property in Pasadena." We gave Stitzel everything we owned there. We were over the moon. He not only took over our properties but also all our debt.

Garry stayed in touch with him until he passed away suddenly a few years later. More than ten years after that, Stitzel's son, by then in his twenties, reached out to Garry and asked for any stories about his dad. Garry told him how much he still appreciated what his father had done for us, how he had saved us when we most needed it.

After we met Doug, Marty came up with the great idea of suing the law firm managing the Pasadena redevelopment—essentially, suing our partners in the project. If we could get some insurance money from them, we could put it toward what we owed the bank. We didn't want to waste our time suing Neil, because he didn't have any money left. His business was ruined, and his company had folded. Instead, we sued the lawyers for the Pasadena project, because what they were doing was not only improper but illegal.

When we went to court for pre-trial depositions, Marty made sure I didn't answer any questions until the end of the day, when he knew I would be tired. When I was asked how the situation was affecting the lives of my family, my children, my parents, I started to cry. The more I talked, the more I cried. By the end, I was sobbing.

Honestly, it felt cathartic to cry. The entire situation was so awful. I did the best I could with the depositions, and then all we could do was wait.

I decided to go to Australia, where Kathleen was living for a short time. It felt good to get out of California while waiting to hear when the trial would begin.

A week or so after I arrived, I was lying in a hotel bed in Sydney when the phone rang. As I picked it up, I could hear Garry crying.

"What is it?" I asked immediately. "What's the matter?"

"There's not going to be a trial," he said.

"What do you mean? We have to go to trial," I said.

"We don't have to," he said.

"Of course we have to. We need to prove that they were not protecting our interests."

"We don't need to do that anymore. They've settled, because your testimony was that good," he told me. "Marty said you were amazing. They don't want to risk going to trial. They are offering us a settlement."

"What kind of settlement?"

"They are going to give us their entire insurance policy," he said. "And you are such a good crier, I think you should cry more in my movies, too."

I was so happy for all of us. After this news, it was difficult being so far from Garry, so I flew back to Los Angeles a few days later.

When we got the insurance money, we gave it all to Bank of America to pay what we owed.

It felt like a huge burden had been lifted, even though we still didn't have much money. After the court settlement, we proceeded to get on with our lives the best we could. For Garry, the entire experience put everything in perspective. He always said that if we lost every penny, he could make more. He had confidence in his writing and directing, and he was never afraid of being out of work.

I would hear rumors and stories about Neil over the years. Dick Cohen died shortly after the firm disbanded, and the employees sued Neil for improper use of their pension fund.

I saw Neil once again before he died in 2005. I was being honored by The Downtown Women's Center, a nonprofit dedicated to finding housing for homeless women. They were honoring another woman on the board as well, and she was good friends with Neil and his wife, Joanne. Many people had known about our troubles with Neil; unfortunately, that didn't keep us from being seated at the same table, right next to Neil and Joanne.

As I looked across the ballroom, I could see them coming in. I told Garry, "Come sit with me. I want us to be sitting together, talking, so we can look him in the eye." We didn't exchange a word. Garry went up to the podium and gave a wonderful speech, as he always did, and we never saw Neil or his wife again. That chapter of our lives was over.

Garry had started directing a new movie, *Beaches*, with Bette Midler and Barbara Hershey. I knew a couple, Johann and Marcella Lau, who were leading a small group to China, and I jumped at the chance to join them. I knew it would not be a trip that would interest Garry. He was not an off-the-beaten-path kind of man. In those days—1988, to be exact—you had to get special permission to enter China. If I was ever going to get there, this was the time and this was the trip.

Johann had lived in China as a child but had not been back since 1945, when he and his parents had had to leave the country in the middle of the night. One of the highlights of our trip was Shanghai.

In 1988, the city was filled with old buildings. We stayed at the city's one nice hotel but could not drink the water that came out of the faucet. Another highlight was Beijing, which we found one of the most modern places we visited. We stayed at a Sheraton hotel, which had a buffet of American food we enjoyed. We visited Tiananmen Square and Chairman Mao's summer cottage in Wuhan. I had never dreamed I would ever get to China, and the entire trip felt very magical and exotic to me.

Garry was not happy about it. He preferred it when I traveled with him; taking a trip on my own felt different and difficult for him. But we both knew that with so many allergies, for him to eat in any foreign country seemed almost dangerous. We had been to Italy and to the south of France with Garry's agent, Joel Cohen (no relation to Dick Cohen), and his wife, Joan. We struggled to figure out how Garry could see more of the world from a more comfortable place than a car or bus or train.

Garry loved playing basketball. In 1992, I flew to Maui to visit him while he was attending Magic Johnson's basketball camp.

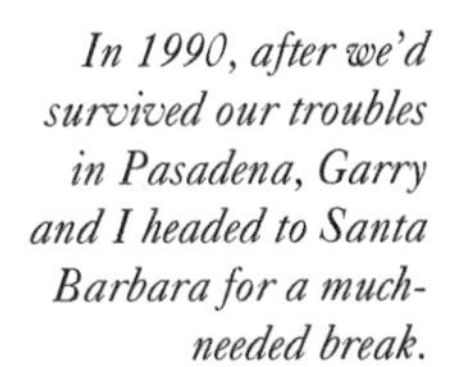

In 1990, after we'd survived our troubles in Pasadena, Garry and I headed to Santa Barbara for a much-needed break.

Garry and I always liked to take small vacations without the children. In 1987, we visited friends at Lake Arrowhead.

CHAPTER TWENTY-THREE

AFTER *BEACHES*, GARRY GOT a new script from Touchstone Pictures, a division of the Walt Disney Studios that released films for older audiences or with mature themes. This script, with the working title *3000*, was certainly dark. It was about a wealthy businessman who pays a prostitute $3,000 to spend a week with him. At the end of that week, he leaves her in the gutter and goes on with his life. It sounded nothing like Garry's other movies, and Touchstone didn't like it much either.

When Garry told me the premise of the story, I looked at him curiously. "That doesn't sound like your kind of movie at all," I said.

"I know," he said. "Not something from the man who created *Happy Days*."

"So are you going to pass, and let someone else direct it?"

"No, I want to do it," he said.

"How?" I asked.

"I'm going to lighten it up," he said. "That's what Touchstone wants me to do. Lighten it up."

3000 went into production in the summer of 1989. Not long after filming started, the producers secured the rights to a Roy Orbison song from 1964, "Oh, Pretty Woman," and the title of the movie changed. It was a small-budget, low-profile film with a relatively unknown young actress named Julia Roberts in the title role. The set was very much below the Hollywood radar, and I think the cast and crew grew close because of that.

During our darkest days, Garry and I had often talked about my going back to work full-time. That option would have forced me to leave the L.A. Free Clinic, and I was so glad it never came to that. I don't think Garry ever really knew what I did there. Ever the hypochondriac, he was nervous about visiting me at the clinic, afraid he might catch a disease. But when *Pretty Woman* began filming, he became interested in the street kids I worked with and started asking me about the young patients. Once Julia was cast, he wondered if she could come to the clinic and do some research.

Garry asked me to find a group of girls to meet with her, saying he would pay each a nominal fee, like $35, to be in a focus group. I found some willing girls and reserved a meeting room at the clinic. Julia showed up in jeans and a T-shirt, looking very similar to the girls from the street. I set everyone up in the meeting room and went back to my desk. About 20 minutes later, I heard someone calling my name from the end of the hall.

"'Bye, Barbara," Julia called. "We're going to take a drive. We'll be back later."

I watched as she left the clinic with a group of street girls and drove off with them in her car. When I realized what had happened, I began to panic and quickly got on the phone.

"Garry," I said. "Unfortunately, your star just left with some of the girls, and I'm guessing they were heading to Hollywood Boulevard."

"Oh, no."

"I think you need to call someone. Does she have a manager? I'm worried," I added. "What if she doesn't come back?"

This was before cell phones, so Garry had to find someone to go look for them. I'm not sure who he called, but I will never forget how scared I was that something might happen to Julia Roberts on my watch. In those days, she was very spontaneous and could move about without any buzz or attention.

Garry spent a lot of time working with her, because the script was very much centered on her story and her growth. He felt she was so young, it was his obligation to not only teach her but protect her.

Richard Gere, who played the businessman, sometimes would lament, "You don't need me in the scene. You just need my suit." But Garry knew how important Richard's character was, as well as how critical his experience would be in helping Julia feel comfortable in her first starring role. Richard had worked for years doing films and plays in Hollywood and New York. He was not only wise but also very grounded, and Garry knew that would also benefit Julia. Richard liked to play piano and was good at it, and that's why Garry added a scene in which Edward plays something for Vivian.

Of course, he spent time with Richard because he wanted him to be happy on the set, too. But he honestly liked Richard, because he is a genuinely nice person. One day, Richard told Garry that he was the same age as his friend the Dalai Lama. Without missing a beat, Garry said, "I think we are both doing pretty well in our fields."

Garry invited me to watch the filming of the big opera scene, where Edward watches Vivian react to a gorgeous performance of *La Traviata*. Opera was never Garry's favorite form of entertainment; whenever I went, I would take my girlfriends instead. The scene was supposed to take place in San Francisco, but filming had been moved back to Los Angeles after the Loma Prieta earthquake, in October 1989, damaged the opera house.

While Garry was shooting that scene, the producers started asking him about the ending. Garry had not yet decided how he wanted to end the movie. I think it was producer Laura Ziskin who said that although Edward changes Vivian's life, he should not rescue her; she should rescue him in some way, to give the movie a modern ending. This led to the final scene on the fire escape, in which Julia climbs down to rescue Richard's character "right back."

The studio didn't plan a big premiere, so when *Pretty Woman* opened, Garry and I went to see it in a movie theater on Wilshire Boulevard that had about six screens. We brought his assistant, Diane Perkins Frazen, and the film's editor, Priscilla Nedd. We were eating in a hamburger place across the street and Garry was getting anxious, so I told him to go with Diane to get our seats. Priscilla and I would finish our burgers, pay the bill, and meet them there.

As I watched them walk out of the restaurant, I noticed a line across the street. "Priscilla, look at that. People are lining up for something," I said. "Let's go see what all the commotion is about."

When we got closer, I could not believe my eyes.

"Oh, my God," I said. "The people are lining up for our movie.

They are here to see *Pretty Woman.*"

The line soon grew around the block. This was not your regular movie. This was going to be a hit, like nothing Garry and I had ever experienced in his career. After the opening weekend, instead of taking *Variety* and *The Hollywood Reporter* from the mailbox and handing them to Garry, I began reading them myself. Every Friday, I would look at that week's gross earnings. *Pretty Woman* was at the top of the list for much of the year. That was the only time I watched the box-office receipts for one of Garry's movies. It was so exciting to know how much audiences loved the film, going to see it again and again.

It would be a few more years before fame changed Julia's life. She and Richard even came to Lori's wedding, at our house in 1989. They danced among the guests on the checkerboard dance floor we'd had constructed on our tennis court. They signed the guest book, ate dinner with our friends, and laughed at Garry's speech.

Garry was always a superstitious person, and I think he believed that in the face of financial ruin, when we had not given up, our reward was earning enough money from *Pretty Woman* to make us feel on top again, financially. He was a man who was always going to be creative, but the fact that he had turned his creative talents into a big-box-office movie gave him great confidence.

Another thing Garry gained from this movie was his long friendship with then–Disney executive Jeffrey Katzenberg. Before filming began, Garry confided his financial troubles to Jeffrey, who not only understood but I think found a way to get Garry some of his money up front, which helped us enormously.

Garry was never one to rest on a success, so he soon went into production on *Frankie and Johnny*, starring Michelle Pfeiffer and Al Pacino. That production did not have the low-key atmosphere of *Pretty Woman.* In fact, it was quite the opposite, because Michelle and Al were big, established movie stars. But Garry was never intimidated by fame or stardom. He used to say he could work with anyone, even someone notorious for being difficult to work with. He just was good with people, and if he could not connect with an actor on one level, he would find another way to do it.

Johnny, Al's character, was a chef at a diner. At the time, Garry and I ate in an Italian restaurant called Vitello's, in Studio City, at least once a week. Our friend Steve Restivo was the owner, and the food was wonderful. They even had a special on the menu called "Pollo Garry Marshall." Before filming began, Garry took Al to Vitello's and had him learn different tricks a chef might know—how to use the various knives or the pans for different sauces. The staff at Vitello's couldn't quite believe it when Al Pacino walked into their kitchen.

Al had a close family friend who was moving into a nursing home, and sometimes he would call me at home to discuss medical questions. That is one thing I think many of Garry's actors had in common: They didn't know a nurse personally, and when they met me, they were excited to be able to ask all sorts of questions. I was always more than happy to answer. I found it a nice way to connect with actors, knowing more about something than they did.

CHAPTER TWENTY-FOUR

AFTER *PRETTY WOMAN*, GARRY and I took a small cruise ship vacation, around the Baltic Sea, and soon realized we had stumbled on something terrific. We could sightsee in every port, but Garry could eat most of his meals on the ship, where the staff knew his food preferences. We didn't have to say, "No vinegar" and "No mustard" every time we walked into a restaurant. The chefs spent a lot of time talking to Garry about his food allergies, and he enjoyed the attention. They welcomed us with a smile and a "Welcome back, Mr. and Mrs. Marshall." Garry always loved being recognized for his directing or acting work, and I loved it when people said his name.

The *Seabourn* was gorgeous and elegant; our cabin even had a private patio. We flew to Copenhagen to board the ship, went to Helsinki and Stockholm along the way, and finished the cruise in London. It was 1990, and *Pretty Woman* was opening all over Europe. I took pictures of the posters in various languages outside the theaters.

One of the places we stopped was a tiny town called Visby, on the island of Gotland, Sweden. Visby is one of the most well-preserved medieval cities in Scandinavia and a popular vacation spot for local tourists. We wandered around the town, and it was just charming. The town had one movie theater, and much to our surprise, *Pretty Woman* was playing there, too. For Garry and me, who grew up relatively poor in the Bronx and Cincinnati, being on a tour of Scandinavia felt very grand. The fact that Garry's hit movie was everywhere we went made it even more remarkable.

The cruise also took us to Russia, where we visited Leningrad, which soon returned to its original name, St. Petersburg. The morning we arrived, I went out to our balcony to watch as our ship moved into the harbor. Garry, who was quite afraid of heights and balconies, came out to see what I was staring at.

"What is it?" he asked. "Don't get too close to the edge; you might fall over."

An army band at the harbor's edge was playing "The Star-Spangled Banner." Garry and I realized that it was the Fourth of July, and they were playing the song especially for the ship's arrival. I think it is the one time that Garry stood on a balcony for more than a minute without being scared of the height. I remember his face, watching the band, and how happy it made him.

When we got off the ship, dozens of local children were waiting to sell us postcards and pencils in exchange for ballpoint pens. I have a picture of me with a little blond boy at the dock. He not only wanted my ballpoint pens, he wanted my heart-shaped diamond necklace. I never take it off. I'm very superstitious about it, because I think it brings me good luck, and the few times I've taken it off, something bad did happen. So now it never comes off.

The little Russian boy just kept pointing to it, desperate to have it. And I just kept shaking my head. "No. You can't have my necklace." That went on so long, we both got the giggles. It was a charming way to enter a city.

Most of our friends in Hollywood were in show business, and it was fun to be with people who were in other businesses. Iris and Bernie Cantor were one of the most interesting couples we met on a cruise. Bernie was the founder of the securities firm Cantor Fitzgerald. At one time, the Cantors owned the largest collection of Rodin sculptures in the world. It was such a small-world way of meeting, because Bernie had grown up in the Bronx, too, and had even attended Garry's high school, DeWitt Clinton. Although Bernie was older than Garry, they had so much to talk about. And I enjoyed getting to know Iris, who I remain friends with to this day.

In Hamburg, the men were offered a tour of the red-light district. When Garry got back, he said that many of the prostitutes were wearing thigh-high boots like Julia wore in *Pretty Woman*. In England, the ship took us up the Thames, and we had breakfast on the deck as we passed under London Bridge. As the trip came to an end, I was sad but also thrilled at the possibilities for Garry and me.

A few years after his death, I found a diary that Garry had kept during this time, and he had written some notes on the cruise. It clearly had an impact on him. At the top of the page, he had written "Favorite Scenes, Views and Moments in the World with Barbara Sue." On the list were these items:

> Copenhagen – listening to the U.S. Air Force band play in Tivoli Square
> Helsinki – buying ice cream in the square
> Stockholm – sitting watching an opera in the old Royal Theatre
> Leningrad/St Petersburg – listening to the Russian marching band on the 4th of July play The Star-Spangled Banner, going to the Hermitage Museum and the Russian Circus

Later that year, we got a call from the public relations director of the Beverly Wilshire Hotel, which was featured in *Pretty Woman*. She said the movie had really boosted business, and the hotel was now offering a *Pretty Woman* package for the ultimate Beverly Hills luxury experience. She invited us to come spend the night and see for ourselves. It was our 29th wedding anniversary, so we decided to take the woman up on her kind and luxurious offer.

The hotel, two-bedroom suite, food, and service were delightful, and we were tickled that Garry's movie had increased business for the hotel. You can imagine how surprised we were when we went to check out and were presented with a bill for $7,000. Apparently, we had misunderstood the PR woman. Garry looked at me like I was crazy, but I told him not to make a fuss and just take out his credit card and pay, which he did.

Now that we knew Garry could eat safely on a cruise ship, we could plan trips just about anywhere. We took a wonderful trip to Alaska with our daughters, as well as cruises around Italy and Greece, to Australia and New Zealand, and on the Tasmanian Sea. Garry was never as happy as he was in Italy, where he adored all the pasta and olive oil. On each trip, the routine of life on a cruise ship seemed to agree with him more. He would unpack his bag for a week or more, eat anything he wanted to, roam about the ship making new friends. When we went out on excursions, the staff would pack safe sandwiches to take with him. At the end of each day, he could sleep in the same bed. He finally felt comfortable traveling, and this increased his desire to travel to countries such as Japan, which had seemed too exotic and scary for him.

Once we returned, Garry would plan another movie, and I would go back to my work at the Los Angeles Free Clinic. Garry was a man who loved working, and I often loved that he did, because it gave me time to be on my own. Sometimes I just liked being home alone, to read a book or watch one of my favorite British mysteries on PBS. I think because I grew up in such a large family, I treasure time and appreciate peace, quiet, even silence. The rhythm felt right for us, doing things together and apart as our three kids finished college and headed off to start their lives.

We could never be gone for too long, because we missed the children and Garry missed work terribly. It didn't matter whether it was a television show or a movie; he just wanted to be working. So sometimes I took trips with the children, and we left Garry at home. One of the most adventurous trips I ever took was with Kathleen, along with my nursing friends Donna Tice and Peggy Giovinazzo, to the Amazon. We flew from Los Angeles to Miami on New Year's Eve 1992 and celebrated the new year on the plane.

We had chosen a photography-based trip, because we liked taking photographs and thought it would involve less hiking than a typical journey. Although we were just bringing point-and-shoot cameras, Peggy, who had been on another photography-based trip, told us most people brought sophisticated cameras and needed time to set up their tripods, so the pace was just right.

The three-week trip began in Quito, Ecuador, from which we took a short flight to Coca, an outpost on the edge of the Amazon jungle. Then we took a 60-mile journey by motorboat down the Rio Napo, a tributary of the Amazon. Our first overnights were at La Selva Jungle Lodge, in the Amazon basin. We stayed in huts that were built off the ground, with no electricity or hot water. It was probably the most rustic trip I will ever take. We'd even had to get shots before we left and bring antibiotics with us.

We had to pack different clothes for the different climates. For the jungle, we brought summer clothing, and for the mountains, winter clothing. When we were in the Amazon, we had to wear thick rubber boots and rain slickers.

In 1993, Kathleen and I went with some friends on a tour of the Amazon basin and the Galapagos. Here we are on the Rio Napo, a tributary of the Amazon.

For the next part of the journey, we dressed more warmly as we explored the Cotopaxi Volcano and National Park, which has been protected as an ecological sanctuary, 14,000 feet above sea level. We stayed at La Cienega, a historic hacienda that once was the center of a huge family estate, originally built in 1580. It was transformed into a country inn in 1981 and is known for its beautiful gardens, restaurants, and special events.

The third week of our trip was spent in the Galapagos. We visited nurseries of fur seals, penguins, pelicans, Blue-Footed Boobies, and

Red-Billed Tropicbirds. At the Charles Darwin Research Station, on Santa Cruz Island, we spent time with huge land tortoises. We also went snorkeling, which was a new sport for me. I usually don't like to get my hair wet, but snorkeling in the Galapagos seemed a once-in-a-lifetime opportunity. When it came to hair, this was not a blow-dryer kind of trip but rather a wash-and-run kind of adventure. In any event, it had started raining as soon as we got off the plane in Quito, and my rain slicker was in my suitcase. My normally smooth, blown-dry hair was pretty much curly and wavy the entire trip.

Early in 1995, Garry launched into an adventure of his own. When they were growing up in New York, his mother had often taken Garry, Ronny, and Penny to the theater, and though they always had the cheapest seats in the house, Garry never forgot the thrill of seeing live plays and musicals. He had always dreamed of owning his own theater; he'd even had a friend draw up some plans. Garry's aspirations had to be put on hold when we had our money troubles, but with the new decade came new hopes, plans, and dreams.

He started by mounting a production of a play called *Wrong Turn at Lungfish*, which he wrote with his colleague Lowell Ganz, with whom Garry had worked on *The Odd Couple*, as well as *Happy Days* and *Laverne & Shirley*. It was the story of a blind and hospitalized man who forms a strong bond with a rough-and-tumble young woman who volunteers as a reader. He debuted the play, a production he directed starring John Mahoney and Laurie Metcalf, in 1990 at Chicago's Steppenwolf Theatre. Working in theater entailed longer hours, less money, and much less publicity than working in film or TV. But to direct words he had written with Lowell and see his work performed on a stage made him happier than I had ever seen him.

Wrong Turn at Lungfish was eventually performed off-Broadway with George C. Scott and Jami Gertz, as well as Tony Danza and Calista Flockhart at different times. Finally, the show moved to a 130-seat performing-arts space in Burbank across the street from the historic Bob's Big Boy, in a theater Garry opened in 1995.

Garry had bought the plot of land in the 1980s from Hollywood legends Ozzy and Harriet Nelson. At the time, it contained three structures: a coffee shop, a small real estate office, and a small auto-body garage. Garry always had plans to build a theater there, but in the meantime, he paid the mortgage each month to the Nelsons, and the businesses paid us rent.

Things changed in 1994, after an earthquake damaged the buildings on the property. The proprietors wanted to rebuild, but the Burbank city administration told them all three structures had to be torn down. I told Garry it was a sign that he was meant to put a theater there, and he thought it was a sign, too.

I was all for it, not only because it was his dream but because it offered an opportunity for him to connect with Kathleen. He had written a memoir with Lori about his career in Hollywood, *Wake Me When It's Funny: How to Break Into Show Business and Stay There*, which was published in 1995. And he had worked with Scott directing music videos and independent films. Kathleen had been a theater major in college and looked forward to building the theater with her dad. He called it the Falcon, after the athletic league he played in when he was growing up in the Bronx. For the rest of his life, Garry produced plays there.

However, the Falcon became a very expensive hobby. From the moment he built the theater, he felt he would need to keep directing movies to support it. *Exit to Eden*, a 1994 comedy-thriller with much of the action in a nudist colony, was not my favorite movie Garry directed. But it certainly made for great research for him and excellent cocktail conversation for me.

CHAPTER TWENTY-FIVE

GARRY WAS THE WRITER in the family, and I was content to leave it that way. There was one time, however, that I borrowed his typewriter, because I had something to say. I wasn't even sure I remembered how to type. But the moment I curled the blank yellow pages around the cylinder and into the machine, my words started flowing. I had a subject and a burning desire to write about it.

My story began shortly after our son, Scott, was born, in 1969. He was our only boy, and the pregnancy and delivery seemed completely typical, just like the births of our two daughters. The doctor said he was allergic to milk, and because of this, he would often throw up through his nose. We took this in stride, because our pediatrician didn't seem too alarmed. Scott adjusted to a soy-milk-based formula, and the vomiting stopped.

No one thought anything else was wrong. As he tried to get his chubby cheeks around his first baby words, he just seemed an adorable little boy.

When he was about two and a half years old, however, I began to worry about him. People seemed to be having trouble understanding his words. Marjorie thought she had the answer: his tonsils. In those days, many people thought removing the tonsils was the cure for all ailments. Every time Garry's mother came to visit, she would say, "Take that kid's tonsils out." Garry told everyone to stop worrying about our soon-to-be-football-playing-hero son.

Scott started nursery school around then. Since Kathleen was just 13 months older than he was, and he would miss her, the preschool agreed to let him start early. It was while he was at preschool that we noticed he had trouble saying hard consonants. For example, the word *car* came out *ar*, and the word *daddy* came out *addy*. He was so cute that it didn't seem to bother anyone, but it started to bother me. I had known a boy in school who had a speech problem, and everyone teased him. I didn't want that to happen to my son. With only a slight mention to Garry, I scheduled a consultation with a speech therapist.

When Scott asked why I was taking him to a new doctor, I told him we were seeing a doctor who could help him say *daddy*. We had been working on this word for months, and the idea of getting professional help seemed to make him happy. I didn't want to talk about it much, because I didn't want to make a big deal out of what could be a minor problem.

The speech therapist had a wonderful selection of toy cars, which were Scott's favorite things. After examining Scott and listening to his speech, the doctor asked if he could put his finger in Scott's mouth. Scott considered this and said, "Yes." The doctor discovered Scott's problem: He had a submucous cleft palate. He suggested we travel to the Robert F. Kennedy Medical Center, in Hawthorne, to see a specialist. I knew we had to face our problems head on and get whatever help we needed, and I was able to get an appointment for the following week.

Then I had to sit down and explain to my sweet, wonderful, hypochondriac husband that there was indeed something wrong with his soon-to-be-football-playing son. He immediately assumed I was wrong. "Why would you take one doctor's opinion?" he asked. Yet he was also leery of taking Scott to another specialist. He felt that if we ignored the problem, Scott would grow out of it. I spent days pleading with Garry to go to the Kennedy Center with us. I felt if he didn't, he would never believe the outcome and verdict.

Garry finally agreed to go with us, and the visit went very well. Scott now knew all the names of his animals, and he wasn't afraid of the doctor. When she asked to put her finger in his mouth, he just opened wide. She felt the cleft in his mouth, too, and she explained the situation to us: When Scott's mouth was forming in utero, the two halves of his mouth did not join properly at the roof. She wanted to take some X-rays. Garry got very quiet, but I felt we finally had a definitive diagnosis and could go about repairing the problem.

Over the next few days, Garry grew depressed, which I think is probably a typical response for a father with no medical background. The X-rays did not go well. Scott was not yet three years old, and here were three large men standing over him in a dark room. I was never far from him, but it still felt scary to him. The doctor had asked him to take a sip of a dark liquid for the X-rays. It tasted so awful, Scott almost had his first fit. But he pulled himself together, clenched his teeth, and dared us to take the X-rays. I asked him if he wanted me to buy him a toy afterward, and he said, "Yes. A Hot Wheel Car."

While Garry felt overwhelmed, I was almost excited, because we would be getting some answers. But when we took Scott to a throat specialist, she noticed in the X-rays that Scott's soft palette seemed thinner than normal. Also, it didn't properly close the passage to the nose, which made him sound quite nasal when he spoke. We realized that was why Scott could never blow out the candles on his birthday cake.

We were left wondering what the treatment options were. The doctor said speech therapy might help, especially since Scott was so young and we had detected the problem so early. When I asked about surgery, she said it was in the experimental stages, but she held out hope for the future.

I have never been one to waste time, so the following week, Scott started speech therapy, three days a week. Since Lori was at elementary school and Kathleen at nursery school until 3 p.m., it was easy to get Scott from his preschool at noon and head straight to speech therapy. I think because I was so matter-of-fact about it, he was, too. I thought we had found the answer to his problem and things would only get better.

However, Scott started to get sick a lot, long colds that went on for weeks and only responded to antibiotics. And then I noticed something odd: Sometimes when I called his name from across the room, he didn't answer me. I thought he was going deaf, and I was afraid to tell Garry for fear he wouldn't believe me. And that is exactly what happened. I told Garry, and he grew angry and said I had better stop finding things wrong with his son. "The next thing you know, you're going to have hearing aids and glasses on Scott."

I said, "I hadn't thought about checking his eyesight, but I will do that after the hearing test is done." This made us both laugh, which broke the tension.

When Garry said Scott's name from across the room with the doctor present, he saw that Scott could not hear him. This was verified by a hearing test. It turned out that Scott had fluid in his ear, which prevented the sound waves from reaching his inner ear. A hearing specialist told us Scott would need surgery to fix this problem: He would insert tiny tubes in Scott's ears, which would allow the fluid to drain.

Before the surgery, we had a family meeting at the dinner table and explained the situation to the girls. We made Scott seem lucky, because we had found a doctor who was going to help him.

We scheduled the operation at a children's hospital where I was allowed to spend the night with Scott both before and after his surgery. Garry gets green from anxiety when he walks into a hospital, so he came the next day. The doctor told us Scott's ears had been very bad, and if we had waited any longer, the surgery would have had to be more extensive.

The benefits of the surgery were almost immediate. When Scott ate his dinner, he said, "What's that noise?" We suddenly realized that he was hearing himself chew for the first time, and it was very exciting.

I covered his ears with paper cups when I washed his hair, and he couldn't dunk his head when he swam, but we got him an inner tube so that he could float in the water. The little tubes fell out twice but were replaced surgically. Scott continued his speech therapy. Over the next few months, things seemed fine.

Scott continued to get colds and sore throats, though, complicating matters. With one throat infection, he got an ear infection, too, and that was the worst thing that could have happened. He developed an allergy to the antibiotic, and the throat surgeon said he needed a tonsillectomy. The problem with this was that after the surgery, Scott would not be able to speak clearly anymore. All the work he'd done in speech therapy would be ruined; but we didn't have a choice, because the colds and infections were hurting his ears. The doctors said after the surgery, we would reevaluate things.

My biggest worry was that in four months, Scott would be starting kindergarten. I began getting a bit depressed about what might happen to my little boy when he met his classmates. Garry and I spent a lot of sleepless nights discussing it. We were happy with our doctors and had to trust that they knew what they were doing. That didn't stop me from worrying that Scott's little classmates would make fun of his speech.

Scott was wonderful throughout this. It gave me encouragement that we had a very bright little boy, who loved talking to the different doctors and nurses about his treatment. He asked lots of questions: How long will I be in the hospital? Will I get ice cream? How long will my throat be sore? In just two short years of doctor visits, he was becoming a pro. What we didn't know is that the next three months would be the hardest of his life so far.

I think we all felt sad as we saw him return to his baby-talk speech patterns now that his tonsils were gone. We were hopeful before our first post-op visit; but when I asked Scott's throat doctor what could be done to help him now, she said there were no surgical options. I was shocked. I had heard of so much being done to help children with cleft palates; why not with a submucous cleft?

The doctor explained that such surgery was available but not for cleft palates as thin as Scott's. I begged her to help us. She gave me a single name: Dr. Gault. I will never forget it, because he saved Scott's future.

Dr. Gault, it turned out, was a specialist in making a prosthesis worn in the mouth that enables normal speech. I was thrilled! I thought I would take Scott to his office, pick up the prosthesis, and we would be on our way! Garry was frightened and I was hopeful, but neither of us had any idea what making a prosthesis that fit perfectly in Scott's mouth would entail.

Dr. Gault described the intricacies of making the prosthesis and worked with our family to make sure Scott would feel comfortable wearing it. He was not sure he would have it done by September, which was my goal. If Scott and I would come to see him almost every day, he told us, he would try his best to finish it before Scott started school.

The process was slow. There were impressions to be made, bands to put on Scott's teeth, a series of X-rays to take, and more appointments to make. Some mornings, Scott could not eat breakfast, because the impressions made him gag. He never cried, though, and was always a very strong boy. He did like all the different children, teenagers, and families we met in the doctor's waiting room during our visits.

When the day to get the prosthesis finally arrived, we knew it would be a long one. Dr. Gault had suggested we plan nothing but this visit for that day. He talked to Garry, Scott, and me for about an hour before he put the prosthesis in. He told us it would take Scott a few minutes to stop gagging, and then he would have trouble controlling his saliva. The nurse gave him a box of Kleenex. Once the prosthesis was in, we were told to take two hours for lunch. Scott could eat something easy, like soup.

I have to admit, during those two hours away from the doctor's office, I did have a sad moment, wondering whether we had done the right thing. Scott seemed so small to be going through all this. At one point during lunch, he cried and asked us to take the prosthesis, or the plate, as we had started to call it, out of his mouth. We managed to distract him through lunch and then took him to a nearby toy store to keep his mind busy. We knew he was trying so hard to keep it together. We promised he would soon feel more comfortable with the plate in his mouth.

By the time we got back to the doctor's office, the saliva problem was gone, and Scott was speaking beautifully. It felt like a miracle,

In 1988, with Scott at the airport, on his way to New York City.

just when we needed one most: Scott started kindergarten in a week. The doctor taught us how to clean and care for the plate and how to safely remove it from Scott's mouth. We, in turn, taught Garry's mother, as well as a close friend of ours who often stayed with the children. We soon included a neighbor and Scott's teacher. Scott was so proud of his plate. He called my parents and his aunts and uncles to show them how clearly he could talk.

Scott walked into kindergarten speaking like a typical child. He couldn't wait to tell his new teacher and friends what was in his mouth. Sadly, Dr. Gault died, but we began seeing a dentist who had trained with him, Dr. Robert Wheeler, who was based in Chicago. He made Scott two more plates, in case one got lost or broken. The plate remained in his mouth for the next 25 years.

One day when Scott was almost 30, he called me with completely unexpected news.

"Mom, can you understand me?" he asked.

"Yes," I said. "Of course. Why?"

"Because I'm not wearing my plate," he said.

We both sat with this fact for a moment. How had this happened? After 25 years, had his cleft palate simply gotten better? When we called Dr. Wheeler in Chicago, we discovered something else. Scott had smoked cigarettes in college, and it turned out that the motion of sucking on the cigarettes had strengthened his mouth. We were all amazed that such a dangerous vice had been responsible for resolving Scott's speech issues.

One of the benefits of raising a child with a developmental problem is that it can bring a family closer, as the members support one another and get through difficult times together. That was certainly the case with Scott. Instead of making him feel different, we surrounded him in an inclusive environment as he played baseball, football, basketball, and even surfed during his high school years. This was an important lesson to have in our past as we moved forward toward welcoming grandchildren into our family.

CHAPTER TWENTY-SIX

ONE OF THE GREAT joys of Garry's life was having grandchildren. I think he was able to relax and enjoy them even more than he did raising his own children, because he didn't have to stress over their careers or ambitions.

Our first grandchildren came into the world three months early, and that surprised everyone, especially Garry. It was June 1995, and Lori was 25 weeks pregnant with twin girls. She and Garry had collaborated on the first of two books, *Wake Me When It's Funny* (the second was *My Happy Days in Hollywood: A Memoir*, published in 2012), and they'd met in Chicago to promote it at a book fair. On the flight back to San Francisco, Lori went into pre-term labor. Her doctor had cleared her for travel, but the twins had other ideas.

Her husband took her straight to the hospital, where she was placed on bed rest for the next ten days. Garry, fearful of anything medical, punched his fist through a wall. Garry's anxiety always spiked around injury and illness, and I had to be calm and collected to counterbalance his mood. I flew to San Francisco to help Lori and keep her entertained.

On June 13, 1995, Lily Camille and Charlotte Grace were born at 26 weeks. The doctors said that while not medically fragile, the girls would have some developmental challenges. This didn't scare me at all, but I knew Garry would be worried about them forever.

Taking care of the girls was difficult, and I flew up to San Francisco so often that when a condo came up for sale in Lori's building, on Washington Street in Pacific Heights, I bought it. I had never owned an apartment by myself, and it seemed a wonderful opportunity to be close to my granddaughters, who were smart and strong despite their developmental delays. After nearly two decades, I retired from the Los Angeles Free Clinic so that I could help with their care.

On Lily's first birthday, she was diagnosed with cerebral palsy.

On their second birthday, Charlotte was also diagnosed with cerebral palsy. It was terribly difficult for Garry to hear, because, growing up such a sick child himself, he worried about the babies being sick, suffering, never making any friends. He feared they would not be able to play any sports, though I explained to him that I hadn't played any sports, and I was fine. They would need physical therapy and some surgery, but they were tough and would soon thrive.

Both girls wore orthotic braces. Garry wore therapeutic braces on his knees for support while playing softball and tennis, so he tried to bond with the girls over their footwear. Charlotte mastered walking on her own, abandoning the metal walker she had used through preschool. While Lily needed a wheelchair, she eventually learned to use a power chair.

I had to teach Garry how not to be nervous around the girls, so we made frequent trips to San Francisco, where he taught them how to throw a ball and to root for their local baseball team, the San Francisco Giants.

Garry, of course, couldn't wait to put his grandchildren in his movies. As with our children, who had done cameos in his television shows, he wanted our grandchildren to be in his films so they could see what he did for a living. The first to do this were Lily and Charlotte, who appeared in his movie *Dear God*, with Greg Kinnear, Laurie Metcalf, Tim Conway, and, of course, Hector Elizondo, Garry's lucky charm and dear friend. Lori was out of town, so their babysitter, Leslie, and I drove them to L.A. The drive was a bit of a nightmare, and the babies were very cranky nearly the entire drive down Highway 5.

Having not yet celebrated their first birthdays, Lily and Charlotte were not impressed with their grandfather's movie career. Once we arrived on the set, their mood grew even worse. When Garry had the prop department spread baby food on their faces, they continued to cry, right on cue. It was not the beginning of an acting career for either girl, but it made Garry very happy to have them on the set, where he could squeeze their cheeks whenever he liked.

Three years later, Lily and Charlotte appeared in *The Other Sister*, starring Juliette Lewis and Diane Keaton. Garry set the story in San Francisco so the twins could visit the set often and be in the movie; Lily and Charlotte appeared with their mother in a parade scene near the end. I spent a lot of time in San Francisco during filming and played a guest at a wedding. I enjoyed meeting Juliette, Diane, and their co-stars Sarah Paulson, Tom Skerritt, and Giovanni Ribisi.

Garry felt *The Other Sister* was one of his best movies. Unfortunately, it was not appreciated by the critics and did not do well at the box office, either. The low box office did not depress Garry but rather challenged him, and he followed up in that year by reuniting Julia Roberts and Richard Gere in *Runaway Bride*.

Garry lamented that they were not getting along as well as they had when they were making *Pretty Woman*, ten years earlier. Shooting a love story was a struggle when his two lead actors were not speaking to each other. One night when Garry couldn't fall asleep, we stayed up in bed talking about it. He said, "How should I shoot them if they won't look each other in the eye?"

I said, "They could fly a kite." Garry thought that was a brilliant idea. He liked seeking my advice because, he told me, I thought like a regular person rather than a Hollywood person. Thanks to me, there is a scene in *Runaway Bride* in which Julia and Richard are watching a kite fly, looking very much in love. Those on the set that day knew they were hardly speaking. Happily, they made up and got along for the rest of the shoot.

The film was set in Baltimore and was an event for the whole family. Lori flew Lily and Charlotte out for their cameos. They appear in a scene in the basement of a church when Julia is running away from one of her grooms. And Baltimore was significant for Lily because she learned to use her manual wheelchair at the harbor. At one point, one of her wheels disengaged and was heading toward the water. Scott saved the day by grabbing it just in time. After we got over the shock, we all laughed hard about the mishap.

Whenever Garry asked the girls what they liked, they would always say, "We like princesses." That was the inspiration for his next movie, *The Princess Diaries*. The best-selling YA novel by Meg Cabot had been optioned by Whitney Houston and producer Debra Martin Chase to make into a film for Walt Disney Pictures. Garry had had a great working relationship with Disney since his days making films for its Touchstone division. He used to say Touchstone was the only place at Disney you could use swear words, as he had in *Pretty Woman*.

Garry set *The Princess Diaries* in San Francisco so that Lily and Charlotte could visit often, which they did. The film felt magical for our family from the day we started talking about the cast. Lily and Charlotte were five years old and heading to kindergarten soon. One weekend when we flew up to see the girls, Garry brought footage from his recent screen tests for the part of Mia Thermopolis. After showing the girls tapes of several different auditions, Garry asked them which actress they liked best to play the princess. Both immediately picked Anne Hathaway.

At the time it seemed an odd choice, because she looked almost Goth, with her long, straight black hair and oyster-white skin, and she'd never appeared in a film before. When Garry asked Charlotte why she liked Anne's audition best, she said, "I like her hair." Garry didn't look any farther.

The stars seemed to align perfectly with the lead casting of Julie Andrews as Queen Clarisse Renaldi. We already knew that Julie had lived in our house while she was making *Mary Poppins* for Disney in 1964. When Garry invited her to the house to meet me, I was impressed that she drove herself, came without an entourage, and wore a baseball hat. She seemed so open and friendly. I served her a bottle of Perrier, and then we walked through the house. She had so many memories of staying there with her young daughter. She admired the beams, the fireplace, the cottage-like feeling. We got to know Julie and her husband, director Blake Edwards, quite well. They were really one of Hollywood's golden couples. Julie is truly one of the most regal and elegant people I have ever met, but she is also very funny and genuine to the core.

Garry cast Kathleen as assistant to the queen. Hector Elizondo played the queen's head of security. Garry put the twins in a scene outside Princess Mia's school, where they played autograph seekers, and I made a cameo appearance as a party guest; Garry gave me a funny line about string cheese. We got to know up-and-coming actresses like Sandra Oh, Mandy Moore, and Heather Matarazzo, too.

It felt like a warm family set, and Lily and Charlotte really got to see what their Pop did for a living. One night, Anne Hathaway even came to their home for dinner, a vegetarian meal, as that was Anne's preference.

We knew the movie would appeal to little girls. Little did we know what a box-office hit it would be in the United States and abroad. Garry followed *The Princess Diaries* with *Raising Helen*, starring Kate Hudson. He felt very nostalgic on that movie, because back in 1987 when he had directed Goldie Hawn in *Overboard*, Kate had been a little girl, sitting on Garry's lap as he directed her mother. He taught her to yell "Action!" and "Cut!"

Lily and Charlotte were in *Raising Helen*, too, as was the rest of our family. Since Garry worked long hours on all his films, he liked having family around, in part because it broke up the day for him. I never thought of myself as an actress, but I felt greater confidence with each movie I appeared in. I enjoyed the banter of the makeup people, the chatting at the catering trucks during lunch breaks, the discussion among the producers in their video village as they watched the filming each day.

I had always looked forward to growing old, and I think for Garry the transition was more difficult. He was very athletic and found great stress relief in playing basketball and softball. When his knees and hips started to age, he grew frustrated with his body, although, despite his many health problems and ailments, he played softball until the end of his life. If he got a hit and his team won, it was a good weekend. If he didn't get a hit and the team lost, his mood grew dark. Just as when he was a little boy growing up in the Bronx, sports and winning mattered.

Right before Garry started *Raising Helen*, he had hip-replacement surgery. This was the first major surgery of his life, and he was scared to death. I, on the other hand, was rather excited, because I knew that afterward, Garry would no longer suffer the pain he had been dealing with for years. He thought he might die during the surgery, while I saw it as a new lease on life. I reminded him that he could still be a hypochondriac, and that I could tell him so because I was still a nurse.

We interviewed several doctors and found a wonderful surgeon who worked out of Santa Monica. Coincidentally, he had just replaced actor James Brolin's hip. The doctor reported that Barbra Streisand had slept on a cot in Brolin's room the entire time. When Garry heard this, he said, "I want you to sleep on a cot like Streisand did and never leave my side, either."

As soon as one of Garry's movies came out, he would cut out all the reviews and put them in a manila envelope. He would not read them for a year. He felt reading them earlier, while he was high coming off the editing of any film that he felt passionate about, would depress him. After a year, he would have the distance to contemplate the reviews and not get his feelings hurt by the negative ones. He worked so hard on each project, and when the critics didn't appreciate one, he was disappointed. The irony is that even when the critics didn't like his films, they usually made money at the box office. And that was Garry's cross to bear—being popular rather than critically acclaimed.

Some men want to retire when they get older, but Garry was not one of those men. Despite the ups and downs, he loved working and he enjoyed making money, especially when he could pour it back into his Falcon Theatre. Looking back on it, the Falcon was Garry's yacht. It was a for-profit venture, so Garry had to direct a movie each year not only to support his family but also to support the theater.

One of his favorite things to do was greeting the patrons before they went in to watch the play. He loved the fact that they recognized him as he welcomed them into a theater he had built from the ground up. For a man who was raised by a tap-dance teacher who loved Broadway musicals, this was the meaning of success—running your own theater and entertaining people. His mother always said the biggest sin was to bore people. To entertain them was to succeed in life. We all agreed that building the Falcon Theatre was a great success for our family.

When Garry wasn't directing a play or a movie such as *The Princess Diaries 2*, *Georgia Rule*, and *Valentine's Day*, we would travel with the children or on our own. I think we had a peaceful rhythm during the last ten years of his life. He often quoted the poet Rainer Maria Rilke, who wrote, "The point of marriage is not to create a quick commonality by tearing down all boundaries; on the contrary, a good marriage is one in which each partner appoints the other to be the guardian of his solitude, and thus they show each other the greatest possible trust."

Relaxing in a park in London, always one of our favorite cities, in 2004.

Garry and I flew to Atlanta in 2007 to celebrate the opening of his film Georgia Rule, *which starred Jane Fonda.*

We threw a big party in 2009 to celebrate Garry's 75th birthday. We filled the lobby of his Falcon Theatre with balloons in shades of purple, his favorite color.

In 2008, we celebrated our wedding anniversary in Las Vegas, where we'd said our marriage vows 45 years earlier.

We flew to Paris in 1999 to promote the opening of Runaway Bride *in Europe.*

CHAPTER TWENTY-SEVEN

EVENTUALLY, WE HAD SIX grandchildren. Scott's children were Sam James, Ethan Garry, and Emma Wells. Having male grandchildren and a granddaughter who lived in Los Angeles made us very happy. Sam became an excellent baseball and basketball player. A year after Garry died, Sam broke both his legs during a very heated high school basketball game. I remember thinking I was glad Garry was gone, because he would have been so angry, he would have probably punched another wall. After the accident, Sam found his way back to sports (and continues to be an excellent athlete), as well as playing violin in the school orchestra.

Ethan and Emma brought great joy to our lives through their love of theater and dance. When Scott's family moved to Malibu, Garry and I would still attend all their games, theater productions, and other school events. We often stayed in our beach house on weekends to spend more time with them. We took them to Dodger Stadium regularly, to Los Angeles Laker games, to see musicals at the Hollywood Bowl and the Los Angeles Music Center. Ethan especially shares my love of theater and often texts me about upcoming musicals he wants to see together.

Kathleen and her husband had a daughter, Siena Jane, named after a city in Italy they love so much. Since they lived just a few blocks from us, Garry grew very close to Siena. She often spent the night at our house when her parents went out to dinner. When Garry started to get sick and had to go to the hospital a lot, we bought her a doctor's lab coat and a stethoscope, with which she pretended to check his vital signs.

All the grandchildren brought great excitement to our lives, with their energy and their different interests and activities. I always knew I would love growing older with Garry, and our grandchildren were the icing on the cake.

For years, Garry liked to say that the key to a long-term marriage was separate bathrooms. This was, of course, a luxury we did not have in the early years of our marriage, and he was very messy, spraying water all over the sink and mirror when he shaved. Several years after we moved into the house on Sarah Street, we remodeled the master bedroom. We found some attic space above the dining room that led to our bedroom, upstairs, and put in a new bathroom, closet, and dressing room just for me. When the remodel was finished, I felt like a princess. It reminds me of the scene in Garry's movie *Overboard* in which Kurt Russell builds a beautiful walk-in closet for Goldie Hawn. Garry and I finally had separate bathrooms, and the distance kept us very happy for many years to come.

So I was surprised to see Garry coming out of his bathroom one morning in the middle of a shave. His face was full of shaving cream and he was still holding his razor. It was late 2009, and he was preparing for his latest film, *Valentine's Day*, to be released in February 2010. He began nervously pointing to a spot on his neck. I couldn't see what he was pointing to because of all the shaving cream.

"What is this?" he asked me.

"What?"

"There is a lump on my neck. I bumped into it when I was shaving," he said.

"I'm sure it is nothing," I said. "Don't worry about it. Get ready and go to work." I gave him a kiss and told him to finish shaving.

He was forever finding bumps, lumps, and bruises on himself and assuming the worst, so I didn't really worry about a bump on his neck. We had been through a few rough years with ailments and injuries, and I knew that as you grow older, things come up and things happen. You go to the doctor, you deal with them, and you move on.

Garry had a series of painful dental implants in 2002, followed by the hip replacement, when I slept beside his bed as Streisand had with Brolin. Whenever Garry had surgery, he was always an excellent patient. Of course, he'd had a lot of practice. He had been sick so often as a boy, he had taught himself how to behave. He did not whine or complain.

Later, he found strength in talking to the doctors and nurses taking care of him. Whenever he met with a doctor or a surgeon, his first question was always "How long until I can play softball again?" Many doctors laughed, thinking it was a joke, but Garry was serious. Returning to softball meant that he was at full strength again. In his later years, he loved playing in a senior softball league in North Hollywood. Each team had a funny name, like the Flatliners or the Cardiac Kids.

Three years after the hip surgery, in 2006, he was diagnosed with prostate cancer. When a hypochondriac hears the word *cancer* for the first time, he immediately prepares for the last rites and a funeral. Garry had been a nervous wreck; but I told him that most men have prostate cancer, and most men do not die of prostate cancer. Of course, I was overstating and generalizing, but I needed him to calm down. A diagnosis of prostate cancer was not the end of the world.

We had to decide how to treat it: with radiation to treat the cancer or surgery to eliminate the cancer. After much discussion, Garry and I chose surgery. I knew what he wanted out of each day, what his schedule was like from the time he woke up until the time he went to bed. He didn't have the time or energy to wade through the sea of radiation treatments. His work was what kept him going, mentally and physically. He had to have the surgery so he would feel confident the cancer was gone and stop worrying about it. I told Garry it was not a big deal, just a routine side effect of aging. I believed that, and eventually, he did, too.

Before any movie, the production company's insurance firm makes the director take a physical. In 2007, one of these routine physicals showed that Garry's carotid artery was clogged. If he didn't have surgery to repair it, he was at risk of a stroke. Garry's surgery was at Cedars, where I had worked when I moved to Los Angeles. I couldn't wait to get him checked out and home again, but time spent in post-op waiting rooms is not torturous to me. I am a very patient person, and I had all three of my children, and my magazines and books and needlepoint, to keep me comfortable. And Garry was back at work and playing softball within a few months.

Now flash forward to 2009, when he felt the lump on his neck. The day before, he had had a random cardiogram, for which dye was injected into his veins. When he was through shaving, I touched the spot he showed me, and it felt like the top of an egg was pushing out of his neck. I thought, "Oh, that's it. He is having an allergic reaction to the dye." Knowing Garry's long list of allergies, this made perfect sense to me. But I couldn't be certain until we got confirmation.

"Why don't you go over and see Dr. Rudnick?" I said. Dr. Paul Rudnick was Garry's primary-care doctor. I didn't think it was anything serious until Dr. Rudnick called me after he examined Garry.

"Barbara," he said. "I think it might be cancer. I need to do a biopsy."

Garry had a biopsy, and the results came back positive.

The lump could not be surgically removed, because it was embedded in the tissue of the throat. The only choice was to radiate the spot, so that is what we did, and the technicians were just wonderful. We made the drive over Laurel Canyon to Cedars at nine a.m., Monday through Friday, for eight long weeks. On Mondays, Garry had radiation and chemotherapy; on the other days, radiation only.

Lori, Kathleen, and Scott wrote him stacks of letters, so that each day we had a new letter to open from one of them. They shared pictures, stories, and memories from their childhood, which helped us smile a lot. And much to our surprise, the radiation and chemo did not make him terribly sick. Garry was, as always, an excellent patient. He took a large dose of Benadryl before each chemo session to help keep him from getting sick, though he did get a little sleepy.

When we finished the chemo and radiation, Garry was ready to direct his next movie, *New Year's Eve*. We had to tell the producers about the cancer treatments, but we didn't tell many other people, including some of our close friends. We didn't want people to worry about Garry more than they needed to, and we didn't want people in the industry to think he was too sick to work. Every time he directed a film, he employed literally hundreds of people, who were counting on him. He didn't want to disappoint the crew, which had worked on so many of his other movies. Garry was a very loyal person that way. He protected and nurtured the careers of people who were kind and attentive to him.

There are moments in your life that you never forget, and one of them for me was when Garry had dental work done, right before he went to New York to start shooting the film. His dentist put a bridge in his mouth on the same side of his face where he'd had the cancer. He would take it out at night to be more comfortable. But when Garry got to New York, he called and said the bridge was rubbing and hurting him. A sore began to form at the site, and it got worse during filming. The radiation had cut off some of the blood supply to that side of his face.

The doctor said we should keep an eye on the sore and hope that it would eventually heal. As I look back on his cancer, it is this bridge that I wish had never been put in his mouth. We didn't know then what we would learn on our own: The sore would never heal.

Only a few people knew how sick Garry was during the filming of *New Year's Eve.* That didn't stop him from having a wonderful time working with stars like Hilary Swank, Halle Berry, and Robert De Niro. Despite the very cold winter in New York, Garry made the set a creative and festive place to visit, as he always did. He asked that I visit more than usual, because he was in so much pain. With me, privately, he could let down his guard and even complain if he wanted to. He trusted me with his health, which for someone like Garry meant a lot.

We always liked to be together on our wedding anniversary, because it was also my birthday. That March, I was 71 years old and we had been married for 47 years. When I got to his hotel, Garry wanted to go out to dinner, some place close, he said, so we could walk and get some fresh air. He always felt invigorated when he stayed in New York City—he liked the streets, the people, and the walking that he did much more than he did in Los Angeles. He loved putting his hat on, bundling up with a scarf, and heading from his hotel room to a nearby restaurant, where the staff usually knew him by name and knew his allergies and food issues.

We walked to one of his favorite Italian restaurants in midtown, and I could see he was tired. He ordered osso buco, and I remember raising an eyebrow at his ordering something so rich and heavy. But I didn't say anything. I knew when he was directing a movie, Garry ate strange things from the craft-services truck. I assumed he was treating himself to a special meal now that I was in town. When the osso buco was served, he started to eat, and suddenly his face fell into his plate. I quickly reached over and lifted his head up.

A doctor sitting at a nearby table came over to help. He took Garry's pulse and said it was weak. The manager of the restaurant called an ambulance, which arrived quickly to take Garry to the hospital. On the way out, the waiter handed me a bill, which I paid and didn't question until later, when I thought it strange to be asked to pay when my husband had just fallen ill.

I explained to the ambulance team that I thought he had just eaten too quickly, but by the time we got to the hospital, they told me they thought Garry was having a heart attack. I didn't think so. Maybe I was in denial, but I wanted to tell them, "I know my husband, and I know what he looks like when he is just not feeling well."

The doctor in the emergency room said he wanted to keep Garry overnight for observation. By this time, Garry had completely rebounded, talking and acting normally. I suspected the whole incident was due to a vasovagal syncope, when some trigger suddenly lowers the blood pressure and causes a patient to faint. It had never happened to Garry, but I had a vasovagal fainting spell once from eating rich food. The doctor was not convinced, and he kept insisting that he wanted Garry to stay until morning.

"You can't possibly keep him overnight," I said. "He is directing a movie, and he has to be on the set first thing Monday morning."

"Are you saying you are taking him out of the hospital AMA?"

asked the doctor, referring to the term "against medical advice."

"I guess I am," I said. "And I've spoken to his doctor in L.A., and he is fine with it."

"Then please let me do one more test, and then you can go," he told me.

The doctor did one more blood test, which determined that Garry had not had a heart attack. He gave me his cell number and said I could call him at any time during the night if Garry felt sick again. Garry always had this effect on doctors. They wanted to help him and see him get better and stay in touch with him by phone.

I called Heather Hall, Garry's assistant, and told her to get a car to come pick us up. I was anxious to get him back to the hotel. I had noticed a film crew shooting a documentary in the emergency room, and I didn't want Garry inadvertently filmed. I was always very protective of his public image and wanted him to be able to work as long as he wanted to. In my mind, the whole incident was just a case of rich food consumed too rapidly. I will never know for sure, but that is what I thought.

CHAPTER TWENTY-EIGHT

THE BIGGER PROBLEM WAS that the sore in Garry's mouth was not healing. When he returned home, we found a special dentist, and I drove Garry to Reseda to see if he could treat the sore. He told us about something called the "French protocol" that might work. By now, Garry had had the sore in his mouth for more than a year, and we were desperate to find a solution. For the next year, he took a series of pills in hopes they would help. But they didn't.

A few different doctors told us that Garry might benefit from hyperbaric oxygen therapy. This involves breathing pure oxygen in a pressurized chamber, like a scuba diver avoiding the bends. In the chamber, the air pressure is increased to three times higher than normal, and the lungs can take in more of the pure oxygen than would be possible at normal air pressure. The blood carries this oxygen throughout the body, where it helps fight bacteria and stimulates stem cells, which promote healing. We found an oxygen chamber in Glendale, just a short drive from our home, and went there several times a week for a few months. Garry continued to work the entire time.

Inside the oxygen chamber, he had to wear nothing but cotton, because fabrics like polyester might spark a fire, so we had to buy him a new cotton wardrobe. He couldn't read a book, because paper could catch fire, too, so we brought DVDs of *Happy Days*, *Laverne & Shirley*, and *The Odd Couple*. We turned them on during his sessions, and he watched from inside the chamber. All the nurses and even other patients getting treatment became very familiar with Garry's television work. It helped us smile and made the time pass quickly as we reminisced about those times and his work.

Unfortunately, the oxygen-chamber therapy didn't make much difference. Garry's primary-care doctor recommended a specialist at the UCLA Medical Center who could scrape his gums in hopes of stimulating them to heal, but that didn't work, either. Having exhausted all the nonsurgical solutions, we scheduled an appointment with Dr. Keith E. Blackwell, another specialist at UCLA, whose practice was devoted to treating head and neck cancers and reconstruction of the head and neck region.

We discovered that he was not only a very nice man but that he had gone to Northwestern, Garry's alma matter, for medical school. Always one to believe in lucky charms, Garry knew instantly that he wanted Dr. Blackwell to perform surgery on his jaw. Anyone who went to Northwestern was a friend of Garry's.

The surgery lasted 12 very long hours. Normally, Dr. Blackwell would remove a muscle attached to a bone in the patient's leg and use that muscle in reconstructing the jaw. Garry did not have sufficient blood supply to that particular muscle and bone, but he did have the proper blood flow in his shoulder, so Dr. Blackwell used a muscle attached to a bone in his shoulder blade, or scapula, to reconstruct the jaw.

When the surgery was over, Garry had a temporary tracheotomy and was not able to talk. This sometimes left him frustrated and angry. We gave him a dry-erase board, which he used to communicate to his friends and family as well as the doctors and nurses. This seemed to make him happier; he sometimes even wrote jokes on the board. I slept at the hospital or in a nearby hotel.

A week or two after Garry was discharged, a nurse came to the house to remove his stitches. I noticed one of the stitches had a little blood on it.

"That one isn't healed up," I said to the nurse.

I didn't want to appear bossy, but the blood looked odd and kind of pussy, which meant the site was infected.

"It will be fine," she said.

When another nurse came to massage his neck and stimulate the jaw, I again noticed blood and pus in the area of the surgery. I called Dr. Blackwell, who put Garry on an antibiotic, since the wound was still bleeding. After the nurse left, Garry got dressed and went back to his office.

About a month later, Kathleen called to tell me Heather was driving Garry home, because he was bleeding from his neck. When they arrived, Heather wanted to call 911. I knew if we called 911, the ambulance would take him to the nearest hospital, which was St. Joseph's. I have nothing against that hospital, but Garry had just had a very specialized surgery, and I wanted him to go back to UCLA Med Center and be seen by Dr. Blackwell's team. Heather drove while I sat in the backseat of the car, pressing a large bath towel to Garry's neck to stop the bleeding.

One of Dr. Blackwell's residents was waiting for us. While we waited for Dr. Blackwell, he told us they would check Garry into the hospital. I had been hoping the doctor would just sew Garry up and let us go home. But he wanted Garry to stay the night for observation. I asked Heather to go across the street to the deli and get us some chicken noodle soup and sandwiches.

About a half-hour later, as I was helping Garry eat some soup, blood started shooting out of his neck, with such force, it sprayed across the examining room. Within five minutes, the hospital team had him on a stretcher heading back into surgery. While Dr. Blackwell travels a lot for work, he happened to be in town that day, and I will be forever grateful for that. I literally signed the consent forms for the surgery with Garry's blood dripping down my arms. I then took a seat in the hospital with my children to wait for the ten-hour surgery to be over.

Garry was discharged with a feeding tube and a PICC (peripherally inserted central catheter) line, and I did not leave my house for the next month. Friends and family brought us meals and groceries. The days felt long and the nights too short. But I tried to stay optimistic and positive for Garry and our children. This was not the end, only a period of recovery that seemed to go on forever. When the feeding tube was out, Garry went back to his office, and I began to breathe again. As 2013 drew to a close, I knew that Garry could have died with each surgery, but he survived, and I was right alongside him to help him recover.

He was dreaming of one last surgery: a knee replacement. His knee was causing him a lot of pain, but he had to be fully recovered from the jaw surgery, and that was not until July 2014. His recovery went quickly, and with the help of a physical therapist, he was playing softball again in no time.

And then he did what he always liked to do: go back to work. After the stress of his jaw surgery and all that time spent at home together, I was looking forward to his directing a movie again, too. I wanted my house back to myself, and to be able to visit him, wherever he was, on the weekends.

A fan sent us this photo, taken in 2016 at the Seattle premiere of Garry's final film, Mother's Day.

Garry looked tired when he began shooting *Mother's Day*, in Atlanta, but his mood brightened as he got to work with such stars as Kate Hudson, Jennifer Aniston, and one of his favorite actresses, Julia Roberts. This marked his fourth movie with Julia, and he put her children, Phin, Hazel, and Henry, in the movie as well. She was a very proud mother as she stood on the set watching Garry direct them.

This was a special movie for me, because Garry surprised me with a gift. I had told him often how I loved the actor Timothy Olyphant, who starred in one of my favorite television shows, *Justified.*

As a present to me, Garry had him play the ex-husband of Jennifer Aniston. I even got to be in a scene with him, playing a nurse. I had twisted my knee a week earlier, but no amount of knee pain was going to stop me from meeting my crush! He was wonderful, and just as cute as I had imagined.

Garry and I went to the premieres in Los Angeles, Seattle, New York, and Chicago, and I have to say we were having the time of our lives. People not only recognized Garry, they also seemed to appreciate him and the fact that he was still directing movies at 81. The press loved interviewing Garry, because he made them laugh. Having been a writer, he enjoyed being interviewed and always told wonderful behind-the-scenes stories about the cast and crew.

Garry was already writing the book for *Pretty Woman, The Musical* while he was working on *Mother's Day*. He had been collaborating with J. F. Lawton, the original screenwriter, to create a stage version. He also was punching up scripts for two sitcoms—a new version of *The Odd Couple*, with Matthew Perry, and *Grandfathered*, with John Stamos—and running his Falcon Theatre. Garry was never one to slow down or be idle, even after surgery. He liked his mind and his body to be busy, filled to the brim with creativity and energy. He only slowed down to spend time in our swimming pool with our grandchildren, who visited often, or during weekends at our beach house together.

Garry was a dreamer, and I was a more practical person. In the spring of 2016, I told Garry that we needed to make a plan to read our wills to the children, to tell them our wishes verbally as well as in writing. Garry said, "Yes, and if you die first, we should prepare them that I will immediately marry a rich woman who knows how to make a great grilled cheese." We both laughed at the thought. Garry didn't even know how to boil water. I was not only the guardian of his solitude but his personal chef as well.

We planned to gather the lawyers and our children during the first week of August 2016. We had no way of knowing that Garry would die three weeks before we could make that happen.

CHAPTER TWENTY-NINE

IN 2008, I WAS standing in line to meet Barak Obama, who was in the middle of his first campaign to become president of the United States. I am a longtime Democrat and have given money to the party as well as to other causes I feel passionate about, such as adolescent healthcare. Garry was always more conservative in his politics, but he was never one to miss a good party. So we were both excited to meet Obama. We were in a very fancy home in Bel Air, and I was wearing a blue suit I had bought for $100 in a dress shop in Louisville, Kentucky, one summer when I was visiting my parents. I didn't let on to any of the other women at the fundraiser that it was not from Neiman's. I wore it with confidence, because it was a beautiful suit.

As we stepped forward to meet Obama, he shook Garry's hand in the most natural way possible, as if greeting a new family friend.

In 2008, we met future president Barak Obama, while he was campaigning in Los Angeles for his first term in office.

"I know you're a great director, but I hear you are a pretty good actor, too." His delivery seemed so relaxed, not at all as if someone had just whispered that tidbit into his earpiece. Garry thought his comment was performed with great comic timing. We posed for a picture with him, and a few months later, he was sworn in as the 44th president of the United States.

Flash forward to 2012, when I'm standing in another line, in another mansion on the west side of Los Angeles, and this time I'm waiting to meet Michelle Obama. My friends Liz and Margo and I moved forward and greeted the first lady, who could not have been nicer. I had decided to wear my $100 blue suit from Kentucky again, because it had looked so good in the pictures with her husband. After we posed for our photograph with Michelle, we started to walk away. Suddenly she tapped me on the shoulder.

"That is a great-looking blue suit, Barbara," she said.

"Thank you. I wore it four years ago when I met your husband," I told her.

She raised her fist in victory.

"That will bring us good luck and we will win again! Thank you!" said the first lady of the United States.

When I was growing up, I never dreamed that I would meet not one but three presidents. (We met Bill Clinton and Jimmy Carter as well.) I never imagined that I would be married to a famous Hollywood director. Sometimes I wondered how I was ever going to get out of Ohio. For me, my life was a fairy tale, and being married to Garry for more than 53 years was a gift. Each year, each month, and each day that I had with him were important to me. Now that he is gone, I can't complain, because I have so much to be grateful for.

Before he died, he had one more project to complete. That's the way Garry talked about life, project to project, with time to relax and bask in between if he could. After the press trip for *Mother's Day*, Garry and J.F. Lawton went back to work on the book for the theatrical, musical version of *Pretty Woman* and planned to start rehearsals in the winter of 2016-2017. They had hired singer-songwriter-composers Bryan Adams and Jim Vallance to write the music, and Paula Wagner to be the producer. Garry knew Paula well, since she is married to his longtime agent Rick Nicita.

They finished writing the book and had started rehearsals in New York City. On Father's Day, we had our children and grandchildren to our house for lunch and swimming. Garry was so happy and looked very relaxed. He liked nothing better than swimming in the pool with his grandchildren. He said it was one of the best weekends ever. On Thursday, he played softball; he pitched the whole game and his team won. Garry was so excited. The following Monday, before he left for work, I reminded him that I was driving out to Malibu that afternoon to watch our grandson Sam play baseball.

"Remember you will be on your own for dinner," I said. "I'm going to eat dinner with Scott and the kids after the game."

"Yes," he said. "I'm going to grab dinner with a friend across from the theater and head home early."

I turned to leave, but he stopped me. "What's wrong?" I asked.

"You didn't give me a kiss," he said.

I smiled and leaned in to kiss him goodbye.

That night, I was driving home from Malibu when I got a phone call from Heather. Garry had suffered a stroke and was being taken to St. Joseph's, the hospital closest to both his office and the theater. I raced over Malibu Canyon Road to get there, nearly beating the ambulance.

The next three weeks were a blur. Garry was in intensive care, and when he woke up, we were able to talk to him. He understood what we were saying, and even got well enough that we could have some of the grandchildren visit. He put on his pitcher's mitt and the kids threw the ball to him. The doctors thought Garry could possibly move to a rehab facility and even home, eventually, with caregivers. I set up an interview with a husband and wife who might be able to provide care for Garry in our home.

We tried to keep him entertained. Lori brought her laptop computer, and we played old episodes of *The Odd Couple*, *Happy Days*, and *Laverne & Shirley* on YouTube. We could tell Garry was alert, because he made a grumpy face when Penny and Cindy came on the screen, reminding him how difficult they'd been to work with.

I slept by his side in the ICU nearly the entire three weeks. One day, I went home to shower and change my clothing while Kathleen stayed at the hospital. Before I drove back, I went into the backyard to sit on a bench near our birdbath. It is surrounded by rose bushes and is one of the places Garry and I liked to be together. Garry always loved a good sturdy bench to sit and reflect on.

Sitting there alone, I started to cry. I was worried that Garry was never going to be the same and that our lives were going to become very hard, much harder than they had been through his cancer treatments. I worried he would be frustrated and angry once he realized he would never be able to play softball again, never have the active life he'd so enjoyed.

But then I wiped my tears. I have never been the type of person to wallow in self-pity. And Garry never liked to see me sad. I thought, "If I'm so sad, I might as well go back to the hospital and be with him and cheer him up."

That night, I entered Garry's room to find a beautiful orchid plant that looked as if it had appeared by magic. It was from Adam Klugman, Jack Klugman's son, with a heartfelt note of hope. How did he know? We had told almost no one that Garry was in the hospital.

Now we started phoning his friends. Many came to visit him, old friends like Ron Howard, Henry Winkler, Anson Williams, Laurie Metcalf, Julia Roberts, and, of course, Hector Elizondo. They didn't hesitate when we called. They just drove to the hospital in their own cars and showed up with hugs.

Garry had touched so many lives, and we believed he would return to us. Our family visits cheered him up and he seemed to be getting better, until he wasn't. The progress stopped. He became unresponsive, and finally, slowly but inevitably, his organs started to shut down.

We met with a very kind palliative-care doctor who told us that Garry's wishes were clearly outlined in his advance healthcare directive. He did not want to be kept alive by artificial means. Garry and I had both signed advance directives, outlining the fact that he wanted to be buried and I wanted to be cremated and have my ashes spread near him. The doctor told the children and me to each take a moment alone with Garry and tell him, "We love you. You love us. We will miss you forever, but we will be okay."

A family picture in 2001, at the Kahala Hotel & Resort in Honolulu. This was our favorite place to go as a family at Christmas time.

With our children and grandchildren at the Kahala Hotel & Resort in 2010. We were big fans of the elevator selfie timer-shot.

Garry's favorite thing to do on Father's Day was to eat dinner with his family on our patio. Here we are in June 2013.

We each took our turns and kissed Garry goodbye. Then the doctor turned off the machines that were keeping him alive, and his soul left this earth, quite peacefully. There was no pain, only quiet and calm. The room was finally silent, and we knew he was gone.

After the private burial in July and the star-studded celebration of his life in November (which Garry would have loved), the children and grandchildren and I made one last Christmas trip to Hawaii. We painted a bunch of rocks purple, his favorite color, and after each of us shared a memory about him, we left the rocks on the shore of his favorite beach near the hotel. Then we said goodbye to the waves he had loved so much and flew home. We would miss him forever, but he would want us to continue to live full lives, just as he had. He would want us to play sports, stay busy, and keep eating fudgesicles, just as he had.

After Garry's death, in the summer of 2016, I sent out one final Christmas card to our family and friends. After years of sending cards every December, I was ready to be done.

It was time to get on with the rest of my life. I started by asking the children to help me clean out Garry's closets. Most people didn't know that Garry was quite a clotheshorse. He had dozens of pairs of shoes, jackets, and elegant ties. Lori took all the ties and sent them with pictures of Garry to some of his closest male friends. At the back of his closet, I found a shoebox with a brand-new pair of the white Velcro sneakers Garry loved, his most comfortable shoes. This made me sad, because I'd buried him in a scuffed-up pair. Had I known there was a new pair, I would have buried him in those. I found myself crying at moments like that, when I was overwhelmed with simply missing him and the way he had made me laugh.

But how could I complain? We had had a wonderful marriage, a terrific life. And now I had to figure out what to do with myself. I'd spent so many years being Garry's caregiver, even putting on his socks in the morning sometimes when he was not able to, that I found I had a lot of time on my hands but plenty of energy, too.

He had specified in his will that he wanted his Falcon Theatre to be renamed the Garry Marshall Theatre and turned into a nonprofit organization. I decided to step in as chairman of the board, a small group that included Kathleen. The problem we faced early on was that Garry had treated the theater like a yacht, pouring hundreds of thousands of dollars into it. He did this by directing a movie every year. Now that he was gone, how were we going to keep it afloat?

After two successful seasons, we are still trying to figure that out. But Garry's dream of bringing live theater to Burbank and the Toluca Lake community is very much a project we will continue working on. I feel passionate about keeping his legacy alive through his theater and other projects.

The other decision I made was to become one of the producers of *Pretty Woman, The Musical.* I felt it was important to become part of the team and help get Garry's story to Broadway. I flew to New York City, became fast friends with the visionary director Jerry Mitchell, and supported the incredible cast, which included Samantha Barks, Andy Karl, Orfeh, and Eric Anderson. I worked alongside J. F. Lawton, who revised the book, as well as Bryan Adams and Jim Vallance, who had written the music.

To help promote the Broadway premiere, I asked a special favor of one of Garry's biggest fans. I asked Julia Roberts if she would come see it with me. She was excited to find out how the movie had been turned into a musical. I waited for her to pull up in a limo with an entourage, but she had none. She was by herself, in a black suit and an orange cotton T-shirt with a picture of *Laverne and Shirley* on it.

"I wanted to wear something that would make Garry laugh," she said. I had to smile. Despite all her fame, she was still the generous and kind person I had met when she was only 21.

After the curtain call, Julia went onstage and met the entire cast and crew, taking candid pictures with them. They were thrilled to meet her, and I was so thankful for her support. It didn't hurt that our photograph was featured in *People* magazine the following week. She sold a lot of tickets that night with her smile.

In 2018, Julia Roberts joined me on Broadway the evening the cast and crew of Pretty Woman, The Musical *honored Garry.*

After Julia helped kick off our musical, *Pretty Woman* ran for a very successful year on Broadway. To see Garry's name on the marquee was to see one of his childhood dreams come true. He had finally made it to Broadway with a hit musical. I have watched the show dozens of times, and I have to say, Garry would have been so proud of the cast and crew and all the hard work they put into it. He would have been thrilled to see the productions in Hamburg, Germany, and London, England, as well.

When the show closed on Broadway, I wanted to thank the cast by giving them mementos from Garry. I gave Samantha Barks a photograph Garry owned of Lucille Ball and Vivian Vance stomping grapes in a famous episode of *I Love Lucy*. (In the movie *Pretty Woman*, there is a scene where Vivian is watching this episode in Edward's hotel suite.) I gave Orfeh a big heart-shaped glass paperweight, one of the last gifts Garry had given to me. Orfeh had been part of the production from the beginning, and Garry had seen her perform in early readings of the script. I gave Eric Anderson and Andy Karl each a pair of cuff links that had belonged to Garry. One was purple, and the other had a design with the comedy and tragedy masks. Love of family, friendship, and loyalty were what he most admired in people, and these four young actors epitomized his values.

Garry might be gone, but he visits me often, as he promised he would do. I was putting the flag out on our front porch for the Fourth of July, which was something we always liked to do together, when two plates fell off the wall. I heard on the news later that there had been a small earthquake, but I knew the falling plates were just Garry's way of saying, "Hello, I'm still here."

Garry thought the biggest sin in life was to be boring. I don't think I had very good comedy timing when I first met him, but over the years he taught me to tell better stories and even make people laugh. I would like to think I taught him how to have a balanced life, even with an extremely successful career in show business. People have been asking me for a while to write my stories down in a book. I am happy to have them in one place for other generations of our family to share. I would like people to know I had a wonderful life and am thankful for all the joy and laughter.

I just knew if I could get out of Cincinnati, I would find happiness, and I did. As I look back on my life, I sometimes wonder how it turned out to be so wonderful. Was it luck? Was it chance? Was it hard work? Was it a combination of things? I can tell you this: If I had married Jack, my life would have turned out differently. Had I not married Garry, it would have turned out differently. Had I not been able to get pregnant the second and third times, it would have been very different. And if I had not become a nurse, I would have not found my profession or, perhaps, come to California. For that, I will forever be grateful to Miss Budke for introducing me to *Cherry Ames, Student Nurse.*

I have no complaints, only happy memories and beautiful children and grandchildren to share them with. If I have learned anything in life, it is to keep on going with a positive attitude. There is no time to be wasted on regrets, only time better spent on happy days ahead.

ACKNOWLEDGMENTS

THANK YOU TO EVERYONE who encouraged me to write my story. I am grateful to Heather Hall, who helped us produce it. I am thankful to Todd Gallopo of Meat and Potatoes, Inc., who designed the cover for us. I am indebted to Pamela Feinsilber, who beautifully edited our words, and Jacqueline Gilman, who designed the interior and helped us navigate independent publishing with such skill. Thank you to Jeff Morris, who supported Lori through every draft and helped us find our title. I would also like to thank photographer Ron Batzdorff, who took my author photo and was a beloved figure on Garry's movie sets. To Cathy Berry and Bruce Wyler: I appreciate you and how you make my life run so smoothly.

None of this would have been possible without Lori, who co-wrote the book, and Kathleen and Scott, who lived it right alongside us on the Dennis the Menace Park paddleboat of life. No one can ever take away our memories of Garry and the love we all shared every time we were together.

Finally, I would like to thank my third-grade teacher, Miss Schneider. She is the one who let me stay in her classroom at lunch and read her leather-bound books. She would be so proud to know that I have finally written a book of my own. May my grandchildren enjoy my stories and pass them down to their own children and grandchildren.

CPSIA information can be obtained
at www.ICGtesting.com
Printed in the USA
BVHW090028140521
607263BV00015B/321/J